THE RESTRUCTURING OF AMERICA:

A Futurist Projection

by

William Merwin

C L A R I T Y

Copyright © 1991 William Merwin

ISBN: 0-932862-13-2

ALL RIGHTS RESERVED. Except for purposes of review, this book may not be copied, stored in any information retrieval system, in whole or in part, without permission in writing from the publishers.

In-house Editor: Diana G. Collier

Cataloguing in Publication Data:

Merwin, William, 1933 -

   The restructuring of America

   ISBN 0-932863-13-2

1. United States - Race relations. 2. United States - Social conditions - 1980 - . 3. United States - Politics and government - 1981- . 4. United States - Economic conditions - 1981I- . I. Title.

E184.A1M4 1991   305.8'00973   C91-097028-9

CLARITY PRESS, INC.
Ste. 469, 3277 Roswell Rd. N.E.
Atlanta, GA. 30305, USA

and

CLARITY INTERNATIONAL
P.O. Box 3144
Windsor, Ont. N8N 2M3, Canada

TABLE OF CONTENTS

FOREWORD

Ravi Patel was born in Aurangabad in 1974 and taken to the United States by his emigrant parents at the age of 12. A graduate of the University of Missouri School of Journalism in 1996, he is now a respected commentator on the American political scene.

He has not, however, forgotten the land of his birth, to which he has traveled many times and in which he lived from 2009 to 2012 as a correspondent for an American news service. While stationed in India to report on India for an American readership, he has also been in much demand for his ability to interpret the confusing events in America for an Indian audience.

As the critical U.S. presidential election of 2016 approached, there was great interest in India in the growing U.S. political and economic crisis. Jawar Gandhi, president of Singh-Gandhi Publishing Co., knowing that Patel had recently written a series of reports in the American press based on extensive interviews with the leaders of the various political movements contending for power at that time, asked him to write a short book summarizing the results of these interviews for Indian readers. The book appeared in India in October 2016, one month before the Presidential election.

The present edition includes not only the text of the 2016 Indian edition (as Part I), but also a new report by Patel on American developments in the seven years since 2016 (Part II).

The Publishers
New Delhi, October 16, 2023

PART I

INTRODUCTION

The American Crisis: One Nation or More Than One?

The American crisis has been building for a long time. Its seeds, in fact, were planted 400 years ago when white colonists decided to bring black slaves from Africa to work the fields. From that time right up to the present century, there have been two main societies in America, separate and unequal, and at least below the surface, the question has always existed: Can these two societies, one black and one white, ever truly be moulded into a single, just, equal and 'color blind' nation?

It is still too early to answer that question, but as the Presidential election of 2016 approaches, many people believe an answer will not be long delayed. Most Americans hope the answer will turn out to be positive, but it seems to this observer that it may be too late, that too many Americans are not prepared to make the fundamental changes in values and institutions required to make this possible. Furthermore, among Americans themselves, there appears to be a growing number of pessimists who fear that the two societies are irrevocably separate and that the political structure of the nation must soon be changed in some manner to reflect that reality. They believe this year's election, with the polarization of positions that has occurred as it approaches, will be a critical factor in determining whether America will move in the direction of a unicultural society where all elements are "melted," or of a society made up of at least two separate and distinct peoples.

The truth today is that the question of national unity is more complex than it was a mere generation ago. This is because the United States has very rapidly become not just a two-society nation, but a three-society one. In fact, the third major ethnic community, Hispanics, recently surpassed blacks as the largest minority population. This shift has been so sudden in historic terms that many Americans even yet have not absorbed its full implications. Their attention has for so long been focused on the black question that the possible threat to national unity posed by a large and growing community speaking a different language has barely had time to enter their consciousness.

Why has 2016 become so critical? Part of the answer goes back to the oil crisis of 2013 and its economic side-effects. The consequences of the scarcity and high price of oil rippled throughout the society and hit particularly hard those whose lives were already economically marginal. This meant, first of all, the minorities, particularly blacks, who had the highest rates of unemployment and were most dependent on the surplus from the broader society and the national economy.

The Oil Emergency of 2013

Steadily declining oil production in Alaska, Mexico, Indonesia, Nigeria, the North Sea and elsewhere finally brought worldwide production below demand in 2013. Commentators the world over quickly realized that the inevitable and long-predicted oil crunch had finally arrived. The oil-importing countries put great pressure on the Persian Gulf countries, particularly Saudi Arabia, to raise production, because this was the only region which could increase output enough to make a real dent in the shortfall. But the Gulf nations refused. They said they didn't want higher production, as they preferred to stretch out their own reserves, which they knew very well were a finite, one-time geological bonanza. Increasing production would not only mean throwing away their own future security, but would not even help the Western world in the long run, they pointed out, as in the end, the importing nations would have to adapt to permanent oil scarcity anyway, and there seemed to be no compelling reason to postpone that day any longer. As one Gulf state oil minister observed, the oil-importing nations " have not used the years since the oil crises of 1973 and 1992 to prepare themselves adequately for the inevitable shift to alternative energy sources, and there is no reason to believe further self-damaging altruism on our part will inspire such action."

The year 2014 saw a 20 percent drop in oil supplies in the U.S. Rationing was instituted, which meant many people were left with inadequate gas to get to work or go shopping, much less take vacations. Anger, fights and gas-line shoot-outs became increasingly common, while gas theft by siphoning became as frequent as shoplifting. A flourishing legal market in ration coupons came into being, supplemented by very sophisticated counterfeiting of coupons. The U.S., where cities had been designed for the convenience of private automobiles, naturally suffered more from the shortages than countries where the cities were less sprawling, in which there was adequate public transportation, and in which citizens were already accustomed to astronomical gasoline prices. On the positive side, a not inconsequential number of Americans showed renewed patience, neighborliness and good humor as they scrambled to arrange car pools for work, shopping and joint vacations.

Nevertheless, no amount of patience or good will could hide the severe economic effects of the oil shortfall. Oil companies were forced to lay off a portion of their work forces, and the impact of the shortfall quickly affected everyone whose work was in any way connected with motor vehicles -- from assembly-line workers and mechanics to gas station owners unable to obtain normal supplies of gasoline and resort operators with no customers. The reduced incomes and buying power of these people -- who constituted perhaps 1/6 of the entire working population -- reverberated through the rest of the economy, affecting the condition even of businesses with no direct connection to automobiles. And of course the higher cost of fuel resulted in high prices for every product which required fuel for its production or transportation -- which meant almost every product sold. What followed can fairly be called a depression, although in order to make a distinction from the 1930's "Great Depression," the recent hard times have generally been referred to as the "Oil Emergency," or simply "the Emergency."

Not surprisingly, those hardest hit by the Emergency have been those on the lowest socio-economic rungs, particularly the minorities. It can be said that by 2013, the black ghettoes were already in a state of permanent near-depression, and the Oil Emergency simply pushed them over the brink into utter economic collapse. When the Emergency's effects hit the ghetto, no level of government -- federal, state or local -- had either the means or the will to offer emergency aid. There was massive resistance among the white population to any increase in welfare, while budget constraints in almost all cities forced school programs, health care and police protection to be cut back. This was particularly true in the ghettoes, which many whites by this time were inclined to write off as beyond help in any case.

The increased distress in the ghettoes exacerbated all the problems of hopelessness, alienation, drugs and street crime. Most whites were already reluctant to enter the ghettoes, and the further decay of these segregated urban islands because of the Oil Emergency made whites even more fearful of them. Blacks who wandered into white areas on the borders of the ghettoes were closely watched, and there were many instances in which touchy whites attacked blacks whom they assumed were up to no good or whom they simply felt had no call to be in white areas. As the already high tension between the white and black communities escalated, the conditions were set for the conflicts which have exploded in the last two years and led to the bitter polarization of the present electoral campaign.

Parties and Leaders, 2016

The present struggle over America's racial and ethnic future can best be understood by looking at three prominent political leaders and the movements they head. They are:

(1) King Dillon, Presidential candidate of the African-American Party (AAP). Plainly the most charismatic of the three, this black nationalist (or African-American nationalist as he would term it, repeating a saying common among his people that black is a *color*, not a *nationality*) has abandoned his former hope that his peoples' future could be found in cooperation with whites. He feels the two races have always been separate and always will be, and the only hope blacks have for bettering their condition is to recognize this "reality" and act upon it. Although Dillon is running for President, it is clear that he has no real expectation of winning. In America, running for President -- provided one has a certain modicum of plausibility as a candidate of nationwide appeal -- is the one way to get maximum media exposure for one's ideas and expand one's following. Dillon has developed into one of the best media manipulators in recent memory.

(2) Andrew Camp, Presidential candidate of the American Freedom Party (AFP). Some see the right-wing AFP as the direct successor to the Republican Party, but it is more complicated than that. AFP backers include many white ethnics in the North and former Southern Democrats as well as former Republicans of the right-wing and Christian fundamentalist wings. (Camp's chief challenger in the coming election will be Sharon West of the New Liberal Party. She does not figure in this book as she and her movement have tried -- generally successfully -- to stay out of the racial and ethnic issues which affect the question of national unity. Her views generally parallel those of the left-wing of the now defunct Democratic Party.)

(3) Manuel Rivera of the Hispanic-American Party (HAP): Unlike Dillon, who has support in black communities in every region of the nation, Rivera's support is concentrated in the southwest tier of states from California to Texas. This being so, he felt that a nation-

wide Presidential campaign would spread his money and time too thinly, and would do little for his political standing in the Southwest. He decided, therefore, to run for the U.S. Senate from California. In that state, Hispanics recently surpassed Anglos as the largest ethnic community, and they should become an absolute majority within a few years. Rivera's electoral prospects depend largely on whether enough of his Hispanic backers can legally register to vote and, if so, will decide to do so. Like Dillon, Rivera argues vigorously that the minorities must win full equality, and soon, if the American union is to remain intact. In Rivera's case, the demand for equality includes equal official status for the Spanish language. Rivera faces Yukio Hashimoto who, by the curious logic of America's most populous state, has come to be known as the "Anglo candidate."

Dillon, Camp and Rivera will each be the subject of a full chapter in the pages that follow.

CHAPTER I

KING DILLON AND THE AFRICAN-AMERICAN PARTY

King Dillon was raised by his unwed mother in the tough ghetto of Chicago's South Side. All he knew about his father was that he was a Vietnam veteran named Isiah Jackson, whom his mother loved deeply but who disappeared into the street life of the ghetto before Dillon was a year old. Jackson had insisted that his son be named for Martin Luther King, Jr., since he was born on the black martyr's birthday. Dillon describes himself as having been a dreamy youngster without goals or direction until his sophomore year at Lincoln High School when the school's basketball coach found him in a state of mild depression over his failure to make the team, and told him he was "lucky because now you can concentrate on something else." Although unconvinced about that, he allowed himself to be talked into conducting some interviews for the school paper, of which the coach was also the advisor. The first interview was with an alderwoman who had graduated from Lincoln; she immediately saw him as a bright young man and, in a three-hour interview, gave him an excellent overview of racial politics in Chicago. The report Dillon wrote (despite some grammatical lapses which he laughed about later) so delighted the coach and so impressed other members of the paper's staff that before long he found himself elected editor. Even more surprising to himself, not to mention his mother, was that he suddenly developed the desire for the first time to actually read his school assignments -- particularly in black literature or related to the role of blacks in American history. In short order his grades went from "D"s to "A's" and he went on to win a National Merit Scholarship.

Dillon decided before high school graduation that he wanted to pursue a career in politics, and became convinced that developing an effective speaking style was the surest way to succeed. Studying law, he had observed, was not only a common route to political position, but also a reasonably efficient means to train one's mind and tongue. So, after compiling an excellent record for four years as a literature major at the University of Illinois, he entered law school there. His determination to develop his speaking style had been demonstrated in his freshman year as an undergraduate, incidentally, when he paid several hundred dollars out of his scholarship and part-time job money to work with a speech therapist. Thus, by the end of the year, he could speak with almost no trace of his original African-American accent. Nevertheless, when he thinks it will help him with ghetto audiences, he can -- and often does -- slide back into this dialect (which, incidentally, most white Americans assume is a product of the ghetto, but which actually stems from *Gullah*, the African-American dialect developed in the south during the time of slavery, which was brought north by the migration of southern blacks in the mid-20th Century. This language is receiving increasing attention from scholars as a distinct African-American language.)

Unlike most of his politically aware black friends during high school and college days, Dillon tended to blame his own race at least as much as whites for their condition. This perspective was no doubt derived in part from the view impressed on him at an early age by his sporadically devout mother that one's fate was in one's own hands. Throughout her life Clara Dillon blamed her own troubles -- from several unwanted pregnancies to drug abuse -- on her own backsliding from the fundamentalist religion instilled in her as a child.

Although Dillon has never completely abandoned this early view that African-Americans are largely to blame for their own problems, he has dropped his mother's somewhat fatalistic religious position that everyone, blacks included, deserves and should accept the punishment that the world inflicts upon them. By the time he was out of law school and working in the Cook County District Attorney's office, Dillon had refined his views into a political line that was both conviction and tactic. His main conclusion was that African-Americans could not passively wait for the white-controlled federal and state governments to solve their problems. Not only did whites lack the will to do so, but equally important, they could not do so even if they had the will. Blacks distrusted whatever programs whites approached them with, and often with good reason, because job-training didn't produce jobs, and attempts at Anglo-like behavior didn't produce acceptance and respect. Anti-drug and anti-crime programs seemed to attack the only way that ghetto blacks had to get a piece of what had long been called "the American dream." And blacks complained that while whites criticized the disintegration of the black family, it was their welfare policies and discrimination on the employment front that helped to promote it. Nonetheless, given the pervasive influence of drugs, crime and family breakdown, it seemed to Dillon, if there was to be any change in their conditions, it could not be brought about without a moral and cultural renaissance within black ghetto society.

At the same time, Dillon recognized that such a renaissance would not in itself be enough, because the black ghettoes did not exist in a vacuum. African-Americans had to have equal educational opportunity; they had to have jobs; they had to have enough real political power to feel their destiny lay primarily in their own hands. And these things could only be won, he felt, with the active participation of whites, for it was the white majority which had created and still controlled the objective conditions under which black society, including its numerically predominant part, ghetto society, existed. According to Dillon, these conditions included territorial encirclement and confinement of blacks to overcrowded ghettoes, control over the creation and location of the great majority of jobs, and de facto residential segregation which prevented true and full job and school integration -- without which African-Americans would never have a fully equal chance in a white-dominated America.

In all the speeches he gave as he began to try his political legs, even when the audiences were exclusively black or white, Dillon always felt that his real audience was both black and white. To become a black spokesman and leader, he felt he had not only to prove he could move black audiences, but also to demonstrate to them that he was a man who could make white America listen. It was his view that blacks would only take him seriously as a national leader if they felt his message was getting through to white America. Therefore, while making it plain to black activists that he shared their discontents and would not shy from confrontation in pursuing full justice and equality, he tried also to convince whites that here was a responsible man who understood their fears of black underclass crime and the spreading cancer of ghetto degradation, and a man with whom they could talk and deal.

By 2008, Dillon felt ready to run for Congress, and he easily won the backing of his district's black establishment, which wanted a candidate who was both a mediagenic vote-getter and an apparent moderate who would not alienate the district's white voters. Elected in a landslide, he was quickly accepted in Washington as an articulate spokesman for black interests -- and not just those in Chicago. He went out of his way to "play the game." He was always restrained, dressed and acted conservatively, and deferred to his congressional seniors in a manner which the latter much appreciated. His TV looks and the fact that he had the ability to explain the black condition in powerful but non-threatening terms made him a favorite on talk shows.

Yet recently some in Congress have claimed they always suspected his overtly deferential manner with his congressional colleagues was not the whole picture. "He sometimes had a certain look," one Georgia representative who knew him for his full seven years in the House told me recently, "which indicated something boiling beneath the surface." This Georgian, who remains on good terms with Dillon personally, claims he wasn't really surprised when Dillon made his dramatic speech last year announcing his resignation from Congress.

This now-famous speech came at a critical moment in black-white relations, as the impact of the Oil Emergency was accelerating the already evident slide of America's inner cities into chaos. The underlying long-term reality behind this slide was a demographic reality which America's cities had never been prepared to accommodate.

Since 1970 the black proportion of the total American population has grown from 10 percent to 15 percent. Of the present (2016) estimated black population of 48 million, about 40 million live in essentially segregated circumstances, with half of that number concentrated in what can fairly be called ghettoes. It is this ghetto environment, and the alienated and destructive underclass which it breeds, which is, and has long been, the chief focal point of racial problems.

Despite the relatively rapid growth of the black population, the number of middle class blacks has, as Dillon often points out, actually been falling since late in the last century. There has, in fact, been a demographic disaster underway in the ghettoes. Even liberals without a racist bone in their bodies admit this. While successful blacks move out and have a very low birth rate, the birth rate has fallen little among those who remain in the ghettoes, and whose lives are characterized by joblessness, poverty, welfare, teenage pregnancy, drugs, broken families, health problems, dropping out of school, and a high propensity toward crime. At the same time, the land area of the ghettoes has grown very slowly because they are surrounded by white areas into which they can expand only through confrontation. Indeed, many of the few black families who have actually managed to obtain housing in white areas have literally been driven from them by the abuse and attacks of their white neighbors. So the ghettoes have become increasingly crowded with people ever less able to compete in, or cope with, the needs of a modern society and economy. Dillon was well aware that such a downward spiral of the ghetto-black condition could not continue forever without causing a social or political explosion. All that was needed was a catalyst, and the economic side effects of the Oil Emergency turned out to be it. The spark that ignited the final explosion of the ghettoes can be said to have been an incident in Detroit involving a truck -- an incident which itself occurred because of the fuel shortage.

The ghettoes were no more dependent on trucking to supply basic needs than was the rest of America, but they had less slack to take up when fuel shortages began to affect the ability of trucks to move goods where needed. Most of the major franchises, food chains and national department stores had not located in the ghettoes for years, and space constraints and fear of theft kept the inventories of the relatively few remaining ghetto stores smaller than elsewhere. Furthermore, residents were less likely to have the private automobiles with which people outside the ghettoes could, if they could find the gas, shop around for scarce items.

The Detroit incident followed a steady buildup of problems in supplying food and other necessities to the ghettoes. The truckers' inability to bring in ample food supplies had already resulted in some of the more mobile blacks going to supermarkets in white areas to shop; a small number had their own cars to drive, while others went by taxi or even by bus, carrying large shopping bags. Occasionally, they bought up all that was available of certain scarce items, which was resented by whites, who responded with bitter looks and hostile words about hoarding. In one nasty incident, black shoppers returned to their cars in a supermarket parking lot to find their tires slashed. Police were called in to guard them and their vehicles while new tires were purchased and installed as a gift from a generous store manager. But with so few ghettoites owning cars, traveling to non-ghetto supermarkets was in no way a solution to ghetto shortages. Supplies got steadily tighter, even as sinking incomes made it harder to buy what was available.

It was in late 2013 that a supermarket-chain truck loaded with groceries was involved in a minor accident at a Detroit ghetto street corner. A gang of black youths took the driver's keys and opened the back of the truck. People rushed to the scene from all over the neighborhood, and within minutes the truck was cleaned out, though the driver fortunately was not hurt. The news of this incident was spread quickly by the media, and before the next night was over, copycat mobs in nine cities had forcibly stopped and robbed grocery trucks.

Truckers responded angrily, many declaring a boycott of ghetto areas. In some cities, police and the National Guard were called in to escort food trucks to ghetto markets, but in a few, truck drivers refused to enter the inner cities even with armed escorts, so the food was actually delivered in National Guard trucks. Nevertheless, it was impossible to deliver all the food needed by these means.

Again it was Detroit on an unusually warm evening in early 2014, where the next stage in the escalation of tensions occurred. A certain black-nationalist leader named Denzil Wright had developed a following of several thousand and, using the common argument that if you had nothing to eat, theft was no crime, he led 600 followers, some on foot and some in cars, toward a shopping center just inside a white neighborhood beyond the informal white-black boundary line. In Wright's parlance, this was to be a "supply raid." A large and angry white crowd watched, uncertain at first as to the purpose of the marchers. While blacks who strayed into white areas were not infrequently followed or questioned by police, this event seemed to have developed with such rapidity that only a solitary police car spotted the marchers and followed them to the shopping center. It was shortly before closing time; the store's management hastily locked the doors. This angered the blacks, who then smashed windows, rushed in and grabbed all they could carry in shopping carts, backpacks and shopping bags. It all happened very quickly. A few more policemen arrived while the blacks were still in the store, but their efforts at control were futile. More reinforcements were called, but by the time they arrived in force, the raiders were heading home. The police were only able to arrest a few unfortunate stragglers, mostly middle-aged women on foot who could not keep up with their younger cohorts. With so few arrests (and those merely on charges of shoplifting, with the perpetrators released immediately on their own recognizance) and no serious injuries, the raid seemed a success to many desperate blacks, and it was quickly copied by others, both in Detroit and elsewhere.

Hundreds of such raids occurred throughout the country, overwhelming the normal police surveillance of blacks venturing into white areas. The police and the National Guard in many cities were kept on a high state of alert, so that they could rush in on short notice to defend stores against raiders, and in a number of cases, easily containable black areas were cordoned off. The police were sometimes successful without the use of force, either through persuasion and support from those black leaders who generally cooperated with the government and were regarded by it as responsible, or because they had marshalled enough men to intimidate the raiders into backing off. In other cases there was gunfire between the law enforcement side and the raiders, who were well armed with everything from Saturday Night specials to automatic rifles which gun enthusiasts, drug dealers and other criminal elements had been accumulating in the ghettoes for years. In some instances, at the pleading of nearby white residents who feared violence in their neighborhoods, outmanned law enforcement personnel stood aside and allowed the raiders to take what they could carry.

The gun battles growing out of the supermarket raids were the opening shots in what can only be described as urban guerrilla warfare. Violence, of course, was hardly new in the ghettoes. Street crime, including a homicide rate several hundred times that in most civilized nations, had become routine, while riots and burnings, which had occurred widely in the 1960's after the assassination of Martin Luther King, Jr., occurred sporadically thereafter, usually in response to alleged police brutality against blacks. Furthermore, ever since the 1980's, a kind of guerrilla warfare had been going on over ghetto turf between drug gangs. These gangs were well-armed with weapons which outside of America would be available only to soldiers on active duty. The toll of these drug-related mini-wars had been rising steadily as the gangs fought over control of what had become by far the most flourishing business in the inner cities.

But in the past, the great majority of this violence had been confined within the ghettoes. With the armed supermarket raids, however, for the first time a substantial quantity of ghetto weapons were being taken, and sometimes used, outside the ghettoes. The symbolic significance of this was enormous. Numbers of desperate and alienated blacks now began to see violence and gunplay not just as a turf battle between black gangs but in larger terms as a struggle of an "oppressed people" against an unjust system. Even some among the most anti-social and criminal elements were receptive to appeals from radical leaders that participating in the raids and doing battle with "the establishment" served the larger political purposes of what the radicals hopefully called "The Revolution."

As racial confrontation and fears mounted, well-armed extremist black nationalist groups sprouted in almost every large ghetto. Typical has been the Black Liberation Army (BLA) in Miami, which has worked very hard to achieve its stated goal of turning that city into the "Beirut of the 21st Century." Comparable situations have developed in many cities, particularly Detroit, New York, Los Angeles and Houston. In other cities, however, the intense fears of violence by people of all races, combined with intelligent political leadership and a bit of luck, has kept violence to levels little higher than the former level of drug-related and street-crime violence.

This writer happened to be assigned to Miami from 2013 to 2015, and was able to observe the growth of the Miami BLA at close quarters. On an April evening in 2014, the police blocked a group of supermarket raiders as part of a law-enforcement policy to contain the ghettoes and soon found themselves under fire from the raiders and their supporters. The National Guard was called in and vigorously hunted down the blacks involved. There was substantial bloodshed on both sides before the Guard withdrew, taking with them a grand total of two prisoners -- both young boys who had not actually been a part of the raid. In the aftermath of this battle, several hundred men and a few women organized themselves into the BLA, which was dedicated to seeking "liberation through armed struggle."

In all probability, the majority of the ghetto populace in Miami and elsewhere has never supported these armed bands, because there has never been any real hope that armed confrontation would topple "the enemy," (that is, the existing power structure) or achieve an integrated, just and equal society. But the armed bands have also known this, it is safe to say. The actual aim of their leaders has probably been no more than to make the cities ungovernable, thereby delivering a supposedly "revolutionary" blow to the existing order. It is by no means the first time on the world scene that an angry population of have-nots has fallen into violence for the sake of violence after giving up hope that it could move the system by peaceful and legal means. Another factor which has probably been of major significance in the formation of the guerrilla bands, though it is little discussed as such, seems to be simply the search for excitement among young men who have no constructive roles to play in society but have ready access to guns. This was also, no doubt, a factor in the Beirut of old as well as in the drug-gang wars in earlier years in American ghettoes.

In some cities, the bands have established de facto control over large sections of the ghettoes. Even residents who oppose armed confrontation with the power structure welcome the fact that some of the bands have either neutralized or absorbed the criminal gangs and independent criminals who ruled the streets before. Where these bands have established control, the main physical danger faced by residents thus ceases to be the random violence perpetrated by the criminal element, and becomes instead the danger of being caught in the crossfire of urban guerrilla battles between the radicals and the authorities. Such battles most often occur when law enforcement agencies or the military send units into the parts of the ghetto controlled by the bands. Although the authorities generally try to avoid such missions because they know they may be resisted by force, they cannot always do so. Never to enter the ghettoes would further lower the already low respect in which law enforcement agencies are held. Therefore, the authorities feel they must risk battle with the guerrilla bands at least occasionally. On more than one occasion, ironically, serious skirmishes have occurred when government troops entered band-controlled areas to help residents by bringing in food and other supplies. Normally the bands would stand aside and not interfere with such efforts, but on these occasions there was apparently a breakdown in communications and the units were attacked.

A constant source of friction in black-white relations in recent decades has been the need for expansion of the ghettoes, and the guerrilla bands have been actively involved in many of the recent conflicts. Even before this decade, ghetto expansion into adjacent areas more often than not caused problems, since it meant that whites felt compelled to move out of well-established homes and neighborhoods. But the guerrilla bands added a new element aimed at speeding up the gradual process of neighborhood "tipping" (i.e. tipping from white or mixed to all-black). The bands decide on an area they feel is ripe for a takeover. They then buy a few pieces of affordable property and turn them into barracks-like rooming houses for band members, while encouraging squatters to move into unoccupied houses. Next they publicly announce that the area is to be "annexed" to the black area, and offer nominal payment for the remaining white properties -- though it is almost always well below what the white residents consider a fair price. Yet the pressure generally works as most whites feel they have little choice. If they refuse the offer, they are likely to suffer, as one guerrilla band leader put it, "the same kind of harassment African-Americans have always suffered when they tried to live in a white neighborhood."

The so-called "Battle of St. Louis" which in May 2015 was seen on television screens around the world, including India, was caused by a ghetto expansion incident involving an unusually radical armed band. Early one morning the band occupied a 40-square-block fringe (i.e. annexable) area in which several hundred whites, mostly retirees, had remained, then tried to escort the white residents out of their homes, promising them payment later. Some old folks who had guns resisted by force, and over 20 deaths resulted. In response to the news coverage of this incident, one black mayor angrily remarked, "Some of the media have totally ignored the legitimate African-American struggle for justice. But now that we have this one incident that presents an unfavorable image of black activists, the media gleefully give it wide coverage. Even the Voice of America, which always plays down domestic violence to make the U.S. look good abroad, has shamelessly played up this unfortunate occurrence."

The Missouri National Guard moved in to drive the raiders out, and the raiders pulled back. But when the governor sent the National Guard into the ghetto in pursuit of the leaders of the raiders, open warfare broke out and lasted for a week. To the surprise of the governor and the military leaders, given the bad impressions created by the TV blitz focusing on the plight of the elderly whites, the ghetto residents gave full support to the guerrillas. There were over 400 casualties by the time a truce was agreed to. Ironically, almost no whites dared move back into their old homes, and black squatters took over a few months later. The former residents have received no payments to date and many probably never will; it may take years for the courts to decide the insurance issues.

Although racial conflict has occurred in big cities throughout the nation, it has generally been more severe in the North than in the South. And in the rural South, where millions of African-Americans still live, there has been very little, relatively speaking. It is reasonable to conclude, therefore, that the current dangerous situation has grown out of the intolerable situation of the urban ghettoes more than from mere contact between people of different skin colors or different cultures.

In parts of the South, the situation is no worse and possibly even better than it was a couple of generations ago. Since the civil rights movement of the 1960's a substantial measure of racial respect and tolerance has been built up in the South, despite the region's heritage of slavery, segregation and blatant racism. Perhaps it is because southern whites know African-Americans belong there, and the latter feel themselves at home. Blacks are spread throughout the South, and people of both races have always been accustomed to contact with each other. This contact may have been -- and may still be -- between master and servant, or "high caste" and "low caste" if you see things from an Indian perspective, but at the least, mere contact doesn't automatically mean conflict. In the North, on the other hand, many whites still consider blacks to be outsiders. African-Americans live in a separate ghetto world which is almost totally outside the daily experience of most whites. It seems as though the preferred solution of many Southern whites to the racial problem would be to "keep the blacks in their place," while that of many northern whites would be to remove them.

Another factor is the somewhat healthier black economic situation in the South, due to the fact that many blacks still live on the land. They have not generally been competitors with white commercial farmers, but they have had their own source of a certain amount of food; those still on the farms at least won't starve. Furthermore, a large number of Southern big-city blacks still have ties to rural relatives, which not only gives some assurance against the extremities of hunger, but also is a not insignificant psychological tie to the land. In fact, since the Emergency began, some recent urban immigrants in the South have returned to the land, choosing a relatively safe rural poverty over the prospects of somewhat higher wages but far greater dangers in the cities. The African-American farms in the South provide at least the nucleus of a viable black economy. It is a long way from self-sufficiency, but it is better than in the cities, where there is almost no significant black economic base at all. This Southern economic foundation is already useful as a cushion, and could become quite important if conditions in the ghettoes cause a growing number of blacks to abandon them. A poor but tolerable subsistence in a predominantly black rural area may not look so bad when set against conditions in America's cities today.

Congressman Dillon's Break with the White Establishment

Like everyone else, Dillon watched with concern the steady descent of the ghettoes into chaos. But he did more than watch. Time after time, he entered crisis situations and attempted to calm passions and save lives. He was not the only black leader to do so, but his high position, mediagenic presence and speaking style that could draw on the accent, rhythms and idiosyncrasies of the African-American dialect (mentioned earlier) made him more effective than most. Yet even as he did it, he must have known that a few speeches and the defusing of a few dangerous situations had little effect on the fundamental realities. No matter how sincere one assumes him to have been in his efforts to calm the inflamed ghettoes, there is no question that (like any politician) he was simultaneously very conscious of the effect his efforts and their media coverage would have on his political future. He was not slow to observe that his involvement was followed closely by the major networks, unlike the efforts of many ghetto activists and other African-Americans recognized by blacks as leaders, and that this created a very considerable political opportunity -- one providing an opening larger than any he was likely to see as merely one of 435 members of The House.

He has not revealed precisely when he decided to resign from Congress and make his move. Perhaps it was a rather sudden inspiration. With the media following his movements daily, and with great hopes being placed by the "white power structure" on his ability to keep the lid on the ghettoes, he could reasonably expect that the dramatic break he contemplated would win immediate nationwide attention and make him the most talked-about black leader in the nation.

Without question, he hoped to win the support of radical black elements which had until then been lukewarm about him because of his reputation as a moderate and his close working relationship with the Congressional establishment; at the same time, for moderates who had applauded his efforts to work within the system, the move would symbolize his own view that this course was now bankrupt.

Dillon waited for an appropriate opportunity to announce his intentions, and found it on June 18, 2015, while the House of Representatives was debating a bill to provide loans to minority businesses in the cities. This was the same sort of proposal that had come up time and again over the previous half century, always with the same result: a few small businesses benefited, many black front companies were created with disguised white ownership, and there was no change in the overall ghetto condition. On this date, members were supposedly limited to five minutes to speak on the subject, but Dillon was sure he would not be cut off by the speaker, Congressman Elwood of Oregon, even if he talked for well over the allotted length and strayed far from the bill under debate. Prior to Dillon's speech, Elwood had worked closely with him and admired him so much that he mentioned him in a short list of trial balloon vice-Presidential prospects.

Dillon began with some perfunctory remarks on the bill under discussion, then quickly shifted to his main theme:

> When I came to Congress, I had high hopes for such bills. I knew that among you were many who favored justice and equal opportunity for all Americans, many who would work for the welfare of my people even though the voters who sent you here might see no direct benefit to them in such efforts. Fellow members, you know I have many friends here. I have always respected and honored you, and still do. The problem is not you, fellow members. Perhaps it is not even the American people you represent -- most of them, anyway. The problem is the system -- a system

which cannot make the wrenching changes needed to give black America what it needs...

Now, what do we need? We do not need more welfare, more gifts, or more efforts by well-intentioned people to solve our problems for us. What we need is a real chance to solve our own problems by ourselves, in our own way. But the present system has put African-Americans in a position from which it is impossible for us to solve our own problems. Oh yes, the mayors of most big cities are black, but in truth they have no power whatever to deal with the real black condition. All they have is the power to play local politics by favoring this group or that, and the power to win a few small favors from Congress for their cities. They have no power to alter the fundamental political and economic conditions that keep African-Americans in poverty, or the fundamental demographic, social and political conditions that keep the ghettoes confined and depressed.

Our present condition will continue for as long as we are part of a society that considers us superfluous, if not an actual hindrance to its prosperity, harmony and safety. It will not change for as long as we are dependent on the generosity of white America for solutions to our problems. It will not change for as long as we lack the political power and the economic resources that will let us build our economic strength from within, rather than wait for some of your surplus to trickle down to us.

For these reasons, I have decided that it is futile to continue my previous role which, let's face it, was one of constantly nagging you to expand your generosity and help. For me to continue in that role in this body would contribute nothing toward solving the real problems of black Americans. Consequently, I have decided to resign from this body and devote myself to building a separate African-American society, because I have come to believe that only this has any real chance of rescuing us.

To my regret, fellow members and friends, this path may in the future sometimes put me in direct confrontation with some of you. I hope you will understand that I have no wish to cut off my personal friendships with you. In fact, I sincerely hope that it will be possible to maintain them. But honesty compels me to acknowledge that the course I have chosen will not be easy or congenial; it will be confrontational and it may become violent. But I see no other way, because our community cannot continue as a powerless, resented and confined semi-colony with no power to determine its future.

What do I mean by a 'separate black society'? As I said a moment ago, to have control over our fate, we must have some measure of real control over our own economic life. And to do this, we will need to achieve meaningful black power in some territory which can be viable in an economic sense. That is to say, we will need to have real political control over something other than the bankrupt cities our African-American mayors have inherited. Many of our black mayors today are excellent people, but presiding powerless over a decayed inner city is not exactly an exalted leadership role. It is at best a figurehead role, at worst a scapegoat role. In our future territory, wherever it is and however large or small it is, we will make our own decisions and take our own knocks. We will suffer many hardships. Like many colonies just after independence, we may for a time become poorer than before. But we will know that if we have the patience, drive and intelligence, we will eventually be able to solve our own problems and build our own future...

Politically, we may need to boycott the present system and choose our own leaders and policies separately, no matter what the present American Constitution may say about that, so that our political life no longer exists merely on the fringes of a system run by and for others...

The first task will be to convince those of our own people who are not yet so convinced that this is the need. Some of my white friends may think that even this will be difficult, if not impossible. But I believe you will be surprised at how quickly the masses of black people will come to recognize the need once it is explained to them. I can assure you, the potential for a separatist black nationalism has long existed. It has awaited only some prospect of its being attainable. Now, as it has been over 62 years since the Supreme Court put an end to official segregation, and yet African-Americans have still not succeeded in being integrated as equals into the American system, and given the unendurable hardship brought upon us by the Emergency, with no remediation whatsoever in sight, I believe the time has come. I intend to dedicate myself to convincing my black brothers and sisters that achieving a separate and meaningful form of black power is our best, in fact our only, hope for the future -- and *that it is attainable.*

How we might acquire the territory and resources that will make our transformation possible, I do not yet know. Nor is it possible at this time to say what political structure will ultimately give us control over our own destinies. However, there are some demographic facts which may become very significant in the coming years. Because of the comparatively high birth rate among blacks in several states of the South, their populations are now about 40% black, and could become over 50% black once again before many years have passed. Thus it appears that African-Americans may be in a political situation before long to control state legislatures. This will hardly mean the millennium has arrived or that our problems will be close to solution. But this demographic reality does indicate that a rather different situation will arise in terms of the real power and real responsibility possessed by African-Americans in those states. The mere fact of having the numbers to make majority decisions through our representatives in the legislatures will force us to exercise significant political responsibility. The existence of black majorities in states with genuine economic bases -- as opposed to cities in a condition of chronic depression -- will create an entirely new political situation for ourselves and, I might add, for white America.

It would be nice to believe that achieving a black majority vote in a few states, combined with a new level of black-white cooperation, would be all it will take to generate the kind of responsible action required to liberate us. This is not impossible;   but neither does it seem to me very likely.

Since the late 1980's there have, of course, been several black governors in the southern states. These have been good men and women, and it is fair to say they did much good for both whites and blacks in their states. But it is also necessary to point out that they could not have gotten elected without large-scale white support, which is to say that they both did not and could not oppose what we might call a white 'agenda' for retaining the existing power structure in the South. In reality, these governors could do nothing that would fundamentally alter the fact that real economic, and therefore political, power in their states was mainly in the hands of whites. The best of these African-American governors were more than mere figureheads, but to the extent that the solution to African-Americans' problems required a significant shift in power relationships, they could do little. The situation will be quite different when black majorities elect not only governors, but also state legislatures, and will have the numbers to insist that their elected leaders put black interests at least on a par with those of whites.

While we may hope for a calm transition to effective African-American majority rule in the southern states, a prudent gambler would not risk a great deal on the chances for it. Populations which suddenly find themselves in the status of minorities due to demographic change do not generally find the transition easy or painless. This has been especially true of whites here and in Africa *vis-à-vis* blacks. Racism is still a potent force in American society today. Most important, even if the transition to black majority rule were to be made peacefully in several southern states, this would still be no solution to the problem of millions of blacks living useless and bitter lives in the ghettoes of the North. The solution to this problem will require a political transformation rather more radical than the gradual attainment of black majorities in the South. In the North we do not belong, never have belonged and never will belong; the only answer to the Northern ghettoes is *to empty them.*

Our grandparents or great-grandparents were told that the North was, relatively speaking, a land of freedom and equal opportunity, and so they went north. But we landed in ghettoes and discovered too late that living in urban ghettoes blocks freedom and equality as surely as living in rural poverty. With the American economy apparently in a state of long-term decline, not to mention the reactionary, racist trend we see becoming even more pronounced in white America today -- represented, if I may say so, by Andrew Camp and his followers -- I see no prospect that conditions in the northern cities will change for the better in the future.

It is the South where our roots are. We have as much right to be there as any white -- perhaps more, because whites have other places, the North or West, which they could consider home. We have no other place. Therefore, I say to blacks living wasted lives in the northern ghettoes, 'It is time to re-migrate to where our roots are, to move south! Help build new black majorities in Mississippi, South Carolina, Georgia, Alabama and Louisiana. If your ancestors in past generations dared to venture into the unknown wilderness of northern cities, how can you fear to head south now, for that means heading home. If you have relatives remaining there, see if they will take you in. If you do not, then go south and find a job, or make a job. Work in the fields. Do anything. Be willing to work for less than the minimum wage if necessary, for those may be the only jobs available if you have no skills. A poor person who has the determination to earn his way in the world is an honorable person, and for him the future will get better. Life may be very hard for a time, but it will be a hardness with hope. Whatever our own near-term individual prospects, we must act for the sake of our children. Once you have resettled in the South, no matter how difficult your circumstances may be, send your children to school and make sure they stay there. Wherever you settle, the state must pay for your children's education, and if your children stay in school and learn, their generation will flourish, because they will have the two things we need to save ourselves -- education and a home. And they will have the votes to make black power a reality.'

You may ask: 'What will the reaction of southern whites be?' I don't know what it will be, but whatever their reaction, it can no longer preclude us from doing what must be done to save ourselves. White greed brought us to this continent. Southern whites wanted us at first, then they were happy to get rid of us as we left for the North. The northern cousins of southern whites put us into the city-wide concentration camps we call ghettoes. Thus, white America *created* the 'black problem,' but it lacks the will or the ability to solve it. Therefore I say: although we should always be willing to work with white America for the good of both communities, we should first of all do what we must to rescue ourselves. We have every right to regather in our southern homeland where our roots are, and we have every right to oppose anyone who tries to stop us. To southern whites we must say: 'If you want to work with us to build a better society, please stay in the South. But you must know that we are coming, for here we belong.'

The South is our future. In a generation we can control the South for the benefit of all who will live there, mostly black but also, we may hope, millions of white compatriots. Our exodus from the northern ghettoes and our rebirth in the South must come.

Let it begin now.

So that's what Dillon called for: a re-migration of African-Americans to the South, leading within a few years to black majorities in at least five states.

As for the political form these states might ultimately take, he left that vague. Based on what he has said since the speech, he does not rule out the prospect that the future black majority states will maintain intact their existing political, economic and cultural ties to the rest of the nation. But neither has he ruled out a far more separate existence for some kind of "black homeland."

The reaction to the speech was not long in coming. Although a mere handful of people saw it live on TV, word spread quickly in the ghettoes. By that night, almost everyone had seen and heard the more salient portions on the news. It is fair to say that Dillon immediately became the most talked-about African-American leader in the nation by far -- this despite the fact that, since his announcement, some of the major white media have tried to minimize his role. But he is definitely "news," so, much as some newspeople would like to play down what Dillon advocates, the TV inclination toward sensation and ratings generally wins, and he continues to be a familiar figure on the evening news. Furthermore, in the black media he is of course seen daily, surrounded by reporters, several major sports figures, and a coterie of volunteer 'bodyguards'. His appeal to black activists is perhaps less the specifics of his "southern strategy" -- which after all has been advocated by proponents as diverse as the Communist Party, The Honorable Elijah Muhammad's Nation of Islam, the Republic of New Afrika and other black nationalist groups in one form or another, from the beginning of the 20th Century right up to this very date -- than the mere fact that here is an African-American leader who snubbed his nose at the white establishment and 'its' Congress. Whatever the African-American in the street thinks about his specific plan, Dillon has acquired enormous potential to move a growing mass of followers -- wherever in the end he chooses to move them.

As for the southern migration plan itself, Dillon has been repeating it over and over to different groups, and there is said to be a lot of talk about it below the surface, among successful middle class blacks, and even in the urban ghettoes where the dream of a black homeland, whether in Africa or America, has always had a following of a kind. There has not, however, been any sign of popular mass migration, at least not yet. Nevertheless, for some decades now there has been a trickle of blacks heading south, and their numbers have reportedly grown since Dillon's speech. If nothing else, Dillon has rekindled a dream. If it takes hold, it will force a dialogue upon white America, a dialogue on the fundamental issues affecting the long-term future of black America as opposed to the monotonous reportage on the daily crises of crime, poverty and sometimes, urban guerrilla warfare, which dominates the race-related news today. In the opinion of this observer, it is a dialogue which is long overdue.

Although at this point no one can predict the outcome of Dillon's plan, it is increasingly clear that the condition of millions of blacks in the ghettoes is intolerable and hopeless. Something must change rather fundamentally. Yet a full-scale 'invasion' of the South by blacks with no homes, no jobs, and no money hardly seems plausible to most Americans today. We know from history, however, that such migrations do occur when people get desperate and they feel they have an alternative place to go. One may recall the Jewish exodus from Europe after Hitler and later from the Soviet Union, or the migrations between India and Pakistan after partition.

It is obvious that a black migration aimed at establishing black majorities would be resented by southern whites. It is equally plain that many would be willing to use force to oppose it. How effective this opposition would be, it is difficult to say. It would, of course, depend both on the strength of white resistance and on the commitment of blacks to the goal in the face of this resistance. Leadership would be critical, and this means Dillon's role would be critical.

CHAPTER 2

ANDREW CAMP OF THE AMERICAN FREEDOM PARTY
(AFP)

The violence in the ghettoes and its spillover into areas outside of them has understandably led to intensified concern among white Americans about racial questions. In growing numbers, they openly express the fear that unless law and order is imposed, the inner city disease will not only worsen, but could come to threaten the stability of the whole society. At the same time, the continuing flood of non-English speaking refugees from Latin American poverty and political revolutions has brought about the widespread belief that unless something is done about immigration, the society will increasingly be fragmented culturally and linguistically, and eventually the political bonds that have kept this diverse nation together may be severed.

Andrew Camp of the AFP has grasped these fears among the white population, and is the only candidate who claims to have a plan for dealing with the conditions that cause them. As the primaries leading to his nomination clearly showed, a large number of white Anglo-Americans agree with him that the first order of business in the cities is to establish order, by whatever means required. As for the immigration question, Camp is gaining a lot of support for his demand to stop immigration almost entirely and forcibly expel illegal aliens.

Camp first made a name for himself as a star quarterback for the University of Pennsylvania football team. There followed a brief professional football career, but he never became a top pro player because of a knee injury which kept holding him back. Unlike many athletes, however, he was fortunate in possessing other saleable attributes: handsome looks and an excellent speaking voice. Television sportscasters liked to interview him, both because they knew viewers enjoyed his "movie-star" quality and because he was always able to make some incisive remark about the sports scene in a well-phrased sentence or two or, when humor was called for, an apt one-liner. Few people were surprised when his agent began to nudge him into a media career as it became clear his playing days were coming to a close.

At first, Camp went into sportscasting, and was good at it -- so good that he became more of a celebrity than most of the athletes on the various Pittsburgh teams he covered. When local sports, business and community groups invited him to speak at their meetings and got to know him better, they picked up numerous clues that not only was he knowledgeable about the batting averages, salary disputes and paternity suits of local athletes, but also that he had certain political inclinations of a rather conservative nature. These were probed further by right-wing community leaders, and before long Camp had been persuaded to do commercials for a political action group called "The Freedom Quest." Camp's friendly visage began to appear in a series of 30-to-60 second TV spots touting the virtues of minimally-regulated free enterprise, low taxes, sharply reduced welfare programs, "law-and-order," the anti-abortion movement and the right to gun ownership; the spots often included fund-raising appeals for organizations and politicians in favor of these causes.

As time went on, the spots gradually became more negatively focused on enemies of these causes, yet they continued to be presented in the same sincere and warm manner that made viewers feel comfortable. His writers included messages against such explicit targets as "environmental extremists," the American Civil Liberties Union, professors and others who wrote things critical of conservative causes, liberals who were alleged to be "soft on black and Hispanic crime," and certain Supreme Court justices and decisions which seemed "out of step with mainstream America," even though the Supreme Court has long been in the hands of justices regarded as holding conservative views. When Camp looked the viewer in the eye and proclaimed in solemn earnestness that a certain politician "will raise your taxes" or "is soft on crime," that politician's standing in the polls was likely to drop several points within the week.

Camp's popular appeal grew steadily, as more and more people who considered themselves conservative came to identify with him as a spokesman. His handlers began to notice that the farther his remarks deviated to the right from what had come to be considered the center, the stronger his backing seemed to become and the more money was brought into the Freedom Quest organization to support its commercials and causes. This response was partly due to the fervor that had always been there on the well-financed right, but also -- as public opinion polls reflected -- because the center, insofar as it reflected white-Anglo opinion, was moving appreciably rightward. By 2004 there was a groundswell of support for Camp to run for office in his native Pennsylvania.

Camp, it turned out, was no fool. Unlike some American politicians who have similarly started out as creatures of the media, he was aware, first, that up to that time he had been mainly a mouthpiece for his handlers and backers, and second, that he had a great deal to learn. True, his general right-wing, anti-welfare state philosophy was pretty well set in concrete. But he could not then have defended his convictions against a good debater -- and he had the sense to realize it.

So as the temptation to respond to the groundswell and seek office began to take hold, he contacted several well-known conservative scholars and told them with genuine humility that he wanted to learn. For over a year, he immersed himself in the classic conservative works recommended to him, and in conversation and debate with his new academic contacts. Although his basic convictions didn't change, by the end of his crash course -- which he liked to describe as "a year of reflection and study" -- he had developed a political philosophy which, whether or not one finds it enlightened, is at least coherent, as well as an effective debating style and an informed feel for the increasingly race-conscious public pulse. During his study year, he continued his Freedom Quest commercials, which by then had already spread throughout the nation, and saw his political support steadily grow.

His first campaign for Congress, in 2006, was successful, thanks in part to large contributions from right-wing backers outside his district. After two terms in the House, he moved on to the Senate in 2010.

Camp's Analysis of the American Condition

In a recent speech before an enthusiastic gathering of AFP supporters, Camp offered his analysis of the American condition. He began by observing that the U.S. had been built by European immigrants and their descendants, and "it would be an injustice to the sons and daughters of Europe to forget it." He continued, "Some may denounce this observation as racist, but I do not at all mean to be racist. There is nothing in this view that precludes full membership in American society for persons of any color or ethnic background. It says only that people of other backgrounds must conform to our fundamental American values -- values which have evolved on this continent out of the heritage of Western civilization -- if they are to be full partners in American society and culture. For us to demand this is, if I may say so, elemental common sense. Otherwise, the values we cherish will be diluted and American society will be fragmented into separate cultures and societies."

"Fundamental American values," he said, include "the use of a common language -- English; the pursuit of the American Dream of prosperity through hard work and free enterprise; economic growth that lifts those at the bottom as well as those at the top; the belief that faith in God is prerequisite to leading a moral life and therefore to good citizenship; and unrelenting opposition to big government and any welfare or collectivist dogmas which once used to be called communism, and now, with the discrediting and abandonment of that pernicious philosophy, are disguising themselves under other names."

As for the question of race -- which despite his constant denials of racism seems to come up whenever his name is mentioned by opponents -- he likes to point out that Americans of Asian extraction have thrown themselves into the American mainstream vigorously and successfully, and he considers them no less American now than someone whose ancestors came from England, Poland or Italy. Furthermore, he notes that some millions of blacks and Hispanics have also become fully assimilated.

His view is, in a nutshell, that it was the immigrants from Europe who founded and built this country, are the primary moulders and custodians of its cultural and social values, and are the creators, owners and protectors of the vast majority of the nation's wealth and property. It is, he tells his enthusiastic audiences, "our country," and "we would be fools to let it be threatened by chaos, crime and revolution spilling out of the ghettoes, or be flooded by immigrants from parts of the world with different values and much lower levels of development -- who are increasingly unwilling even to learn our language."

Camp is willing to admit that the ultimate blame for ghetto conditions belongs to whites:

> It was whites who brought slaves to this country and kept them in oppression for centuries. Furthermore, whites continued blatantly to discriminate against blacks for a century or more, even after the end of slavery. But for the last half century, the problem has not been one of discrimination. It has been the inability of black America to put its own house in order. Blacks say they want to participate in the

American Dream. Fine. Many have already done so; but too many haven't. Too many have sunk into their ghettoes where they breed recklessly and expect productive Americans to bail them out with welfare to alleviate the consequences of their own irresponsibility. Millions of ghetto blacks have taken the paths of crime and drugs rather than fight their way toward success in our free and open system. Yes, millions. In a black male population of some 23 million {2015 estimate}, over four million have spent or will spend time in jail.

We all know that there are bad elements in every ethnic community. But within the black ghetto underclass there is an entire subculture of pathological behavior. It is a subculture in which hard work, self-reliance, family solidarity and respect for law and morals are no longer assumed to be the societal norms. It is a society In which the majority of babies -- in some cities, 70 percent -- are born out of wedlock; in which one in five men spends time in jail -- a rate seven times that of white Americans, which itself is, we must regretfully admit, higher than in any other industrialized society. It is a society in which, in some cities, 60% don't finish high school. Again, this subculture does not represent the dreams and efforts of the nationwide majority of blacks. But it is an underclass subculture sufficiently large and widespread that its impact on the broader American society appears to many other Americans to outweigh the successes and contributions of the black majority. When we consider the role of blacks in America in 2016, it is the problems created by this disruptive underclass subculture which most readily come to mind, not the aspirations and achievements of millions of solid, upright black citizens. And it is this dangerous underclass which must be blamed for the fact that the black community, taken as a whole, has not yet achieved full and equal partnership in America.

Black apologists say their situation is different from that of other ethnic groups. Only blacks must overcome the stigma of institutionalized slavery and second-class citizenship, they say. Yes, this is true. But America is a country of immigrants, and no group achieved prosperity easily. All who succeeded had to fight with intelligence and hard work to find their place in the sun. Nor are blacks the only minority that has suffered unfair treatment in the past in America. Look at the discrimination suffered in the past by Jews and Chinese, for instance. Do black apologists claim that those minorities had it easy? Far from it. Those minorities achieved success by working harder than the rest of us until they caught up. I say to blacks sunk in the ghetto culture, If the challenge you face is greater, then you must struggle all the harder. It is true that you will have to work harder for success than I or my children. That may not be fair, but it is the reality; and it is a reality that others -- including many individual blacks -- have faced with determination and success. The plain fact is: either you make that tougher fight for a generation or two, or you sink deeper into despair and chaos. Let me add this: if you want to transform your community, we will help you. We look forward to the day when the black community restores sound education, revives the strong family system blacks once had, and takes full advantage of the free economic system we have in America. We eagerly await that day, for if we are truly to achieve the American dream for all, there is no alternative. There is plainly no other place for you to go. You can't go 'back' to Africa any more than we whites could solve our problems by going 'back' to Europe. But if you do not choose to make the extra effort required to save yourselves, then we will take whatever steps may be necessary to prevent the destructive ghetto subculture -- which has now spawned an armed rebellion -- from threatening the values and well-being of the rest of us.

Camp has said his policy toward the ghettoes will employ a "carrot and stick" approach. That is, as in the above quoted speech, he tells African-Americans that if they transform the ghetto subculture, they will be welcomed as full and equal partners in America. Yet he has said in private that, at least for the near future, he is not confident that ghetto communities have the will to rebuild the ghettoes and ghetto society. He notes that for decades there have been groups such as the Black Muslims -- about which he has said some surprisingly positive things -- that have been trying to salvage the ghettoes, but these groups have been fighting a losing battle against the easy way out of succumbing to welfare, drugs, casual violence, the "street hustle," hopelessness and intellectual laziness. Seeing little hope that this situation will soon change, Camp says that there will probably be no choice but to apply the "stick" more than the "carrot." As he put it in another recent campaign speech: "We say to those who live in the ghettoes: We are going to maintain law and order in our cities. If the present chaos and violence in the ghettoes continue, we will, once I'm elected, institute martial law."

Whether or not Camp considers himself a racist, the things he has said during this campaign have certainly struck many African-Americans (and others) as sounding racist. Among those who follow Camp's remarks with more than casual interest is King Dillon. Dillon has publicly castigated Camp and said that any attempt to use the military to control the ghettoes will mean "civil war." But I know from talking to Dillon that in fact he welcomes Camp's movement. First of all, on one basic point -- that African-American salvation must come from within the African-American community -- he actually agrees with Camp. But of no less importance to Dillon is the mere fact that Camp's movement has helped bring the racial issue to a head.

Dillon has come to the view that there must be a polarization of racial tensions in America, because without it people, both black and white, will continue to opt for the easy way out -- that is, to sit back, express good intentions, and hope for the best -- whereas what is needed is to shake the very foundations of the system. The isolation, anger and hopelessness of the ghettoes are so severe, Dillon believes, that a wholly new, "revolutionary" approach is needed -- thus his proposed black takeover of the South. "Revolutionary changes do not occur when people continue to feel they can muddle through," he told me, "and a direct confrontation between the minority African-American and the majority Anglo-American population will be an essential ingredient in persuading both parties that they can no longer muddle through."

Yet another reason Dillon welcomes Camp's movement is his belief that to many people in the U.S. and abroad, Camp's movement will appear so blatantly racist that when the ultimate confrontation comes, African-Americans will receive a great deal of sympathy and support, both domestic and foreign. It is Dillon's opinion that world public opinion is a most important factor in aiding the achievement of African-Americans' goals, and limiting the range of administration actions against African-American movements, because of America's increasing recognition of its interdependence with and need of support from other nations. The achievement of majority rule in Azania and the anti-western Islamic movement represent new cards in the play of world forces which Dillon views as likely to be favorable to his cause.

Andrew Camp has recently had to do some delicate ideological gymnastics in regard to demographic questions. As a dedicated supporter of right-wing causes, he originally and in all sincerity aligned himself with the anti-abortion movement, but his position began to change as he pondered the high illegitimacy rate among ghetto blacks -- a rate that would, he knows, be far higher if abortions were outlawed, since over half of the illegitimate pregnancies are aborted. A few years ago, the religious right from which he gets much of his support would have abandoned him in droves if he had wavered on abortion. Fortunately for him, however, there has been a shift on the right concerning this issue in the last few years.

For some decades now, the black population has been growing at about twice the rate of the white (while the Hispanic growth rate -- thanks largely to immigration -- has been about twice that of blacks). As the minorities have grown rapidly as a percentage of the total population, the concerns of many whites about the ultimate political and economic ramifications of this demographic shift have pushed moral qualms about abortion into the background. The more the far right considered the long-term socio-economic costs if all those unwanted pregnancies became unwanted children, the less it was inclined to hold to its original anti-abortion, "pro-life" stance. A large percentage of the non-aborted births would have been to unwed mothers with little means of support and certain to raise their children at public expense in the worst conceivable ghetto conditions. It might be noted that in some urban black communities, where abortions exceed live births and fewer than 40% of the live births are legitimate, outlawing abortion would have meant that fewer than 20% of births would have been to married couples that wanted the child.

Perhaps Camp did lose a few votes when he shifted his own position and came out openly in favor of full government funding for abortions for any woman unable to pay, but the main effect of his shift has probably been to lend legitimacy to the already growing view among the right-wing that it is morally acceptable after all to support abortion as an aspect of public policy while still being faithful to the rest of the conservative cause. Camp very cleverly managed to persuade a couple of well-known TV preachers to publicly proclaim a willingness to accept abortion at the same time he was making his own changed position known. It may be noted also that on the abortion issue, he agrees with Sharon West of the New Liberal Party, though for different reasons. West sees abortion as a right of free choice for women and an essential part of a population limitation policy designed to decrease pressure on resources and the environment, while Camp worries that the fate of the nation will be ever downhill if in each generation the people who are "unable to prosper in, or even cope with, the needs of American society in the 21st Century" (a rather transparent coded description of the ghetto "underclass," which itself is often used as a coded description for African-Americans) produce more children while "productive citizens" have fewer.

The Hispanic Question

The relationship between blacks and whites has traditionally been the primary minority question in America. Yet African-Americans, who now number 48 million, have been surpassed in numbers by the 56 million Hispanics. In Camp's view, the "Hispanic question" is less a racial than a linguistic one. What disturbs him is the fact that a large and rapidly growing segment of the Hispanic community now uses Spanish almost exclusively, and that even among young people there are many who are no longer motivated to learn English. This also disturbs many other Anglos, it seems.

Within the last few years, a "critical mass" seems to have emerged in terms of the creation of a separate Hispanic sub-society which can function in all spheres of life without English; and this linguistically separate society is growing very rapidly due both to continued massive immigration from Latin America and the high birth rate among Hispanics, the majority of whom are immigrants or descendants of immigrants over the last 60 years. Plainly, without this historically recent immigration, such a separate non-English-speaking society would not have arisen.

During the campaign, Camp has said almost as much about the immigration question as he has about the ghetto underclass. His basic position is that immigration should be ended altogether, except for a small number of refugee cases and the reuniting of immediate family members of legal American citizens who have been separated across international boundaries for reasons beyond their control. In reality, given the present relatively low birthrate among white Anglo-Americans, Camp would probably be willing to see more immigration

from Europe. Few people, however, now care to leave the compara-
tive prosperity and security of Europe to emigrate to the U.S.. Camp
knows there is no reasonable basis in justice for allowing in the few
Europeans who want to come while keeping out millions of others,
particularly Latin Americans; so the only fair way to keep out the
multitudes from south of the border is to restrict immigration across
the board.

For a few years at the end of the last century, the U.S. seemed
to be getting a grip on the immigration issue. In the late 1980's, the
government had passed an immigration bill containing amnesty provi-
sions for over two million illegal aliens combined with employer
sanctions against hiring ineligible illegals. The control effort seemed
to work to some extent, but was always threatened by the fact that
illegals were willing to work for even lower wages than their legalized
compatriots, and provided business with a more compliant labor
force. Attempts in the 1990's to satisfy business and keep Hispanic
labor south of the border, through free trade with Mexico, were only
partially successful. The number of workers hired by companies that
moved to Mexico was small compared to the number pulled north by
opportunities in the U.S.. Furthermore, since the whole purpose of
moving these businesses south of the border was to benefit from
low-cost labor, wages could not be raised above a certain level.
Consequently, the dream of finding greener pastures north of the
border did not die. In the last two decades, immigration policy has
once again fallen victim to the inability of the ethnically pluralistic
American population and the government which represents it to
agree upon and carry out a cohesive, long-term immigration policy
that would offend no major group. It must be admitted, however, that
even a united and determined government would have found it difficult to stem the ever-growing flow of refugees from the runaway
population growth in Latin America and the resulting poverty and
revolutions.

The granting of legal status through the amnesty program to
great numbers of people who had entered illegally made it very hard
later to convince potential immigrants that the U.S. had both the will
and the means to control its borders over the long term. Millions in
Latin America, Asia and elsewhere reasoned that, provided they
could enter the U.S. (which was easy), find an inconspicuous job and
lay low for a few years, there was a good chance that they too would
be covered in future amnesties. As a Yale law professor said of the
immigration situation back in the 1980's: "Beating the system has
become a game -- and is widely recognized as such by all concerned.

It is a game, moreover, that almost any resourceful alien equipped with easily obtainable fraudulent documents or a competent lawyer can easily play." (FAIR Immigration Report, Nov. 1987.) Those who counted on future amnesties were, not surprisingly, vindicated. Amnesty continued to be the government's "easy way out" -- far easier in the short term than an effort to round up and deport millions through massive raids by immigration authorities on areas of heavy alien concentration.

In the end, the amnesty and employer sanction policy created little more than a blip in the tide of immigration. In fact, amnesty itself led directly to the arrival of many millions of new immigrants, as those with newly-won legal status were now able to bring in family members.

In recent years, fraudulent documents have become so common and so sophisticated that no small-business employer could be expected to verify the legal status of those seeking employment. Most employers have hired anyone they wanted who had plausible-looking documents, and taken the attitude that it is up to the INS to come and check out the documents. Employers could always argue -- frequently quite honestly -- that they employed applicants in good faith, having no reason or means to doubt the validity of their documents. The INS has simply been overwhelmed by the number of aliens -- legal and illegal -- holding jobs, and can't begin to check more than a small fraction.

Although Hispanics now outnumber African-Americans nation-wide, they can not so easily be seen as a single ethnic group, either culturally or politically. The successful Cuban-American professional or businessman, for instance, sees his interests aligned much more with Anglo-America than with poor, uneducated Mexican farm workers. Nor does a Puerto Rican in a New York City ghetto necessarily identify with the farm worker, even though both are poor; the Puerto Rican's interests, in the political arena at least, are much closer to those of African-Americans and other urban minorities trying to survive amidst inner city violence and joblessness. Thus, whereas blacks have only two identities (American and African, in a rather generalized sense), Hispanics tend to have three (American, Spanish-speaking -- whether bilingual or monolingual -- and Cuban, Mexican, Puerto Rican or wherever else they or their parents came from).

Consequently, when Camp talks about the growing Spanish-speaking population and sees in it "the seeds of a threat to national unity," he is not referring to the nationwide 56-million strong Hispanic population, but to the predominantly Mexican concentration in the states along the border with Mexico. In Camp's view, it is this concentration -- containing, in addition to the Mexicans, growing millions of immigrants from Central and South America -- which has created a "population so large and culturally distinct from the rest of America that it is bound in the long run to develop separate and distinct political interests."

By now there are areas in the Southwest where the descendants of post-World War II immigrants are into the second or third generation of Spanish usage, despite great efforts to teach English in the schools. While it is true that even in these areas, the majority do still learn English, a growing number feel that English is only marginally useful; they know they can get along using Spanish exclusively, whereas they certainly could not get by in the areas where they live using English only. Although all states require on paper that English be used for schooling beyond the earliest grades, it is reported that many schools, even through high school, have in the last few years used Spanish more than English. This is not a plot initiated by Hispanic school administrators, but simply an accommodation to reality; where people neither need to nor are able to handle English well, there is no point in talking at them in English. With Spanish, you may not be helping students to integrate into the broader American society, but at least you are able to give them a basic education. This situation is rather new, having arisen only in the last decade. It is directly related to the question of a "critical mass," mentioned above -- that is, a "population mass" of Spanish-speakers large enough and concentrated enough to constitute a fully-functioning society in which Spanish is more useful overall than English.

While the majority of Hispanics even in the Southwest almost certainly still do favor learning English as a second language, some radicals are now urging their people to abandon English altogether. Nevertheless, the recent decline of English is due far more to the practical linguistic demands of everyday life than to appeals from radical Hispanic nationalists. In any case, the decreasing commitment to English can only add fuel to Camp's anti-immigration stand -- as well as to the separatist fires that Manuel Rivera is busily fanning.

For the last few years, Rivera's following has been growing rapidly in the predominantly Hispanic parts of the Southwest states. These include the southern parts of California, Texas and Arizona, and most of New Mexico, plus those counties of Colorado just across the New Mexican border. In the last two decades, these areas --

totalling about 7% of the territory of the U.S., or an area slightly larger than France -- have shifted fundamentally in demographic and cultural terms. Culturally, socially and politically, they are now more Hispanic than Anglo. There is some question as to whether Spanish is already the most commonly used language in these areas, but none as to whether it will soon become so. Even economically, Hispanic interests are the most visible on the streets, although the majority of large enterprises and most of the land still belongs to Anglos. Hispanic nationalists like Rivera are quite vocal about their determination to change the latter reality.

It should be pointed out that southern Florida, the other major region with an Hispanic majority, is in quite a different situation. The Hispanic population there is primarily Cuban, and it continues to see its destiny more closely tied to the Anglo states to the north than to the Mexican-American states far to the west. This will probably continue to be true even if Hispanics eventually become the largest population in the entire state.

Andrew Camp professes himself to be a "friend of Hispanic America." He has emphasized that Hispanics arrived in the Southwest long before Anglos did, and he has no quarrel with Hispanic American families which in his view have a "legitimate historical and legal right to be in America." What he attacks is the large-scale illegal immigration of the last half-century or so which "threatens fundamentally to alter American society," and the massive illegalities that have occurred in conjunction with that immigration -- including falsification of documents, drug smuggling and a widespread tendency to see those trying to enforce immigration law, and by extension any law, as the enemy. He has spoken frequently and in some detail about how he intends to deal with illegal immigrants and illegal immigration. The United States must immediately implement a system of absolutely foolproof photographic and fingerprint identification cards, he says, adding that every person shown to have no legal right to be in the United States should be deported, by force if necessary, to his or her country of origin. Of course, a policy of forced expulsion has been on the books for decades, but insofar as it concerns Mexicans, it has had little success, as a large proportion of the deported illegals simply try again another day. Camp has said his administration will "not shrink from the expenses or consequences of examining all naturalization cases all the way back to the original amnesty bill of 1987, and in any cases where fraud is found, citizenship or residence status will be revoked." (However, even some of his most fervent supporters question whether such an effort will be possible.)

"Control of our borders," Camp said on another occasion, "is no less important than a war for national security, and under my administration will be pursued with equal energy and resources."

While acknowledging that some Hispanic Americans will undoubtedly feel harassed by a vigorous pass system, Camp says his administration will do everything possible to insure that no one faces intrusions on his or her civil rights beyond the inconvenience of having to prove legal status. In justifying this and other policies to Hispanics, Camp argues that they will never achieve equality until they are integrated into "mainstream" (his code word for "Anglo-American") American society; and that they will never become fully integrated until they adopt English as their primary language, accept strict controls on immigration, and control their population growth to the extent that other population groups no longer feel threatened by overly rapid demographic change. Therefore, Camp contends, for the Hispanic community to accept his immigration policies will in reality be in its long-term interest.

Camp hopes to confirm English as the sole official language of the nation, to be used exclusively in all governmental publications and activities, including public education. These policies, he concedes, will have to be phased-in gradually, allowing time for non-English speakers to learn English. He emphasizes that he is not against foreign language learning and competence. In fact, he would favor any activities that promote other languages as second languages. The teaching of languages in schools, the showing of foreign movies and TV programs, and the effort of families to retain immigrant language traditions at home could all be seen as part of a legitimate second language effort, he says.

Although he knows the reaction of Hispanics to his language policy will be unfavorable (to put it mildly), Camp says that without it, national unity will be increasingly threatened, given the close tie between language and the other factors -- cultural, social, political and economic -- also pushing toward separatism. He argues that, combined with all these other factors, a separate language forms a barrier which is making the gap between a growing portion of the Hispanic community and the rest of the nation unbridgeable. Language alone need not do it, he says, pointing to Belgium and Switzerland, among those countries which have maintained political unity despite linguistic diversity. But in none of those countries does the language difference coincide with such clearly defined cultural and class distinctions. He observed in a recent speech: "Look at the problems Canada has had because the citizens of one province,

Quebec, speak French, while those of the rest of the nation speak English. There continues to be a strong Quebec independence movement, and there is no guarantee that national unity can be maintained over the long run. Yet in reality, the differences between French-speaking and English-speaking Canadians are minuscule. They are about equal in economic well-being; they look identical for all practical purposes; and there is no fear by either side that the rapid population growth of the other is in any way a threat to their own territorial harmony, cultural values or political interests. Compare this to the present situation of Anglos and Hispanics along our Southwestern border."

Thus, the two issues that Andrew Camp is emphasizing in this year's campaign are the breakdown of order in the inner cities and the perceived threat of a national split along linguistic lines. These are, in his words, "the most serious internal problems we have faced since the Civil War." In his view, the former problem justifies martial law, if necessary, to maintain order, while the latter justifies tight limits and controls on immigration. Based on recent polls showing Camp far ahead in the Presidential race, it appears a great number of Americans have come to agree with him.

CHAPTER 3

MANUEL RIVERA OF THE HISPANIC-AMERICAN PARTY
(HAP)

Since readers in India have long known of the problems of blacks in America, it is easy for them to understand the anger and aspirations behind King Dillon and his movement. But the situation is different with regard to Hispanics, about whom little was heard until recently. The HAP's Manual Rivera may seem to Indian readers to have come out of nowhere, claiming to represent a population larger than most European countries. The fact that Rivera is running merely for senator from California rather than for President should not be taken to mean that his influence is felt only in that state, important as it is.

Manuel Rivera comes from an old Mexican family known to have settled in southern California in the 1790's. There is no indication that the family was ever rich or prominent, but the myth has come down from generation to generation that his ancestors were a proud and contented people for generations until the Anglos arrived in the mid-19th Century -- and it has been downhill ever since. Rivera himself grew up on the mean barrio streets of East Los Angeles, where the common assumption among his peers was that Anglo-imposed inequality and injustice were the ultimate cause of the poverty, crime and drug abuse that pervaded the barrio.

The family myths and the evil street environment nourished in Rivera an intense discontent with the status quo and animosity towards the existing -- i.e. Anglo-dominated -- political and economic power structure. As with many other radically-inclined Hispanic youths, he sympathized with such "anti-Yankee" left-wing regimes as those of Cuba and Nicaragua. During one phase, he tried in his own political dialogue to force American realities into the Marxist categories he half-understood from the writings of Latin American radicals. But this phase didn't last long, as he quickly came to realize that in the U.S., while Marxist class analysis might not be entirely irrelevant, you couldn't understand the problems of Hispanics if you ignored racial, cultural and linguistic differences. (Note: Although the terms "Hispanic" and "Latino" are both used for the minority population discussed in this chapter, the former is now more common and is used here; it is also more inclusive -- covering Cubans, Puerto Ricans and other Spanish-speaking or Spanish-surnamed Americans as well as those of Mexican extraction. "Latino" tends to be used primarily for the Mexican-American population. Rivera himself uses both terms.)

Although Rivera has not entirely abandoned the views of his youth, he now has a more mature perspective. He no longer blames Anglos for every difficulty or defeat suffered by Hispanics. He acknowledges, in fact, that the historic inability of Hispanics to organize a coherent and dynamic political movement, as well as their sometimes less than adept grasp on the levers of economic advancement, have not infrequently made them their own worst enemy.

Nevertheless, despite the necessity on political grounds to work with Anglos on many questions in his home state of California, Rivera, like King Dillon, sees some form of separatist Hispanic-power movement as an inevitable part of the "true liberation" of Hispanics. And this is bound to mean, he says, a political confrontation with Anglo-America. He acknowledges that his may still be a minority view among Hispanics: "As with most peoples, probably only a minority of Hispanics spend much time pondering the underlying political causes of their condition. I'm sure the majority are just interested in obtaining the comfortable life of the American Dream which they see on their TV sets. But I do think a growing number are frustrated at our inability to achieve full equality within the American system, and feel the system must be changed fundamentally."

As to what he meant by "liberation," he explained: "... either full equality in an integrated America or some form of separate existence for Hispanics." He added, "Unfortunately the chances for real integration and equality seem to be receding rapidly -- particularly with the emergence of Andrew Camp." As for his definition of "a separate existence for Hispanics," he said it plainly would require a certain territory in which Hispanic culture and political influence would be predominant, and in which Spanish would be the dominant -- even the official -- language. Whatever form this territory might take, Rivera says he is certain of one thing: "History provides full justification for an Hispanic claim to the southwestern part of American territory."

This history is particularly important to Rivera -- and it is no accident that he majored in history and taught the subject in high school before running for the California Senate eight years ago. His original career choice was, he has explained, a direct outgrowth of his experience in the barrio, with its poverty in such sharp contrast to the comfortable prosperity he saw as he passed through other parts of the city. "How did it happen," he wondered, "that although we were here first, we lost everything -- the land, our political power, our language?" When he voiced such questions to his elders, he got no answer except the bald statement that "the Anglos took everything." I remember asking him once when discussing the immigration question if he couldn't understand how present-day Anglos might be disturbed when they see their neighborhoods overrun by immigrants from Latin America, and he responded, "How do you think my ancestors felt when they saw Anglo immigrants take all the land after the Mexican War?"

Rivera set his mind on becoming a teacher so he could show young Hispanics how their condition came to be, how unjust it was and how, in the long sweep of history, it could and -- if they did what they must -- would change. One result of his lifetime immersion in history has been the growth of a time perspective shared by few other Americans, particularly politicians. While most Americans seem to figure their problems are something to be faced and hopefully solved by the next election, Rivera, in an almost Chinese way, deals in decades and even centuries. The present situation of Hispanics in America is the result of 200 years of history, he says, and he would not shy from the cause of "Hispanic liberation" even if he thought it would take another 200 years to achieve it. But of course his actual timetable is a lot shorter than that.

There is no question that Rivera is sincere in claiming that history justifies a strong sense of Hispanic grievance as well as a dominant place for the Spanish language and Hispanic culture in the American Southwest. An Anglo historian who is a friend of Rivera recently summarized that history in an article published in a Los Angeles daily:

> Spanish settlement of the Southwest began at the end of the 16th Century, with Santa Fe being founded in 1610, ten years before Plymouth Rock. Settlement in Texas began before 1700, and California began to be occupied in the middle of the 1700's. Although the number of settlers was small, the fact is the Spanish had exerted their claim to the region and backed it up by settlement for well over 200 years before the young American republic began to feel the irresistible pull of Manifest Destiny. The Americans quite understandably believed that the Spaniards -- and after Mexican independence in 1821, the Mexicans -- were not putting this vast land to good use. Not only was settlement sparse, but control from Mexico City was also very

weak. And when the Americans convinced themselves they had a right to take the land, the resistance put up by the Mexicans was negligible, as wars go. Although by the standards of a later age, the American acquisition would have been seen as a plain case of imperialist aggression, Americans of the time felt the young nation marching toward the Pacific was perfectly justified in pushing aside the loose and inept Mexican rule. One may guess that most people abroad -- those who had heard of the war at all -- probably agreed. As to what the Mexican residents of the territory thought, no one seems to have given that much thought. Probably a majority didn't oppose American rule once it was established. Their first interest was no doubt in the economic well-being of themselves and their families, so their dominant feeling probably was one of hope that under the conspicuously energetic Americans, life would improve.

Rivera often proclaims his conclusion from history that the U.S. stole the Southwest from Mexico by force and that it had no moral right to do so. That is not the only way to see it, but it is easy to see how someone who is engaged in an Hispanic nationalist political struggle would feel justified in latching onto this chapter of history as a weapon. He has very little difficulty in selling the argument to anyone inclined to see present-day Hispanics as unfairly disadvantaged. He has somewhat more difficulty in rationalizing the fact that the original citizens of Mexico and their descendants were so quiet politically for nearly a century and a half after the territory was "stolen."

After the Southwest was annexed by the U.S., there was a sudden influx of Anglo-Americans, who quickly became the dominant population. The Hispanic population numbered perhaps 100,000 at the time of the Mexican War, with slightly over half in New Mexico, and it is unlikely that it grew much, if at all, from then until the Mexican Revolution in 1910. In the following decade, some 1,000,000 Mexicans came north to escape the armed strife and to seek work, but at least a third of this number returned to Mexico during the 1930's depression. Thus by World War II, there were fewer than 1,000,000 Mexicans or Mexican-Americans in the U.S.. The labor shortages which resulted from the war brought in a substantial influx, but it is unlikely that by 1960 the Mexican-American population exceeded 4 million in an overall Hispanic population of perhaps 6 million. Since Hispanics were also the poorest and most powerless element in the population of the Southwest, it is not too surprising that little was heard from or about them at that time. There was little risk to a politician in simply ignoring the interests of Hispanics.

The big demographic change came with renewed large-scale immigration in the 1960's, especially after the passage of a new immigration law in 1965. Opening the doors to immigration, especially from non-European areas, can be said to have been a generous impulse of the new civil rights era. Open-hearted Americans were determined to show that in regard to race they were, as they said, "color-blind" -- and anyone who talked of limiting Mexican or other non-European immigration ended up sounding to liberal ears like something of a racist bigot. Also, it was felt by many Americans that, with so much of the rest of the world suffering from overpopulation and political turmoil, it was only proper for the U.S. to do its share to alleviate world conditions by allowing more people to immigrate to the U.S. -- which, after all, seemed to have lots of room compared to much of the overcrowded Third World. Since there was then no widespread awareness among Americans of the long-term ecological ramifications of overpopulation, there was little effort to limit immigration on these grounds. Having descended from immigrants themselves, Americans have always felt uncomfortable in saying, "Now that we are here, let's close the door on any more immigrants." Finally, it cannot be overlooked that American business benefited mightily from the rock bottom wages that it was able to pay to such immigrant populations, using them to hold down wage demands by Anglo laborers, and to do work that members of the dominant population had come to avoid.

The result was that legal immigration grew from 250,000 per year in the 1950's to 600,000 in the 1980's. The increase for *legal* immigration from Mexico seems relatively modest -- from around 40,000 per year in the 1960's to something over 70,000 in the late 1980's. Nevertheless, this was enough to help create a growing Mexican population in the region, and thereby make it easier for the truly massive influx of illegals to melt inconspicuously into the population.

With immigration out of control, the Hispanic population grew rapidly, more than doubling from 9 million in 1970 to 21 million in 1990 (not including non-amnestied illegal aliens, for whom estimates ranged from 2 million to 8 million.) During the same 20-year period, the black population grew by something over 30% while white-Anglos grew by approximately 10%.

Immigration has had yet another important impact on the Hispanic community in the Southwest. If it hadn't been for the influx of Mexicans and others on the lowest socio-economic rungs, the Hispanic community might now have achieved, or be well on its way to achieving, full integration and equality. There was already movement toward better education and middle class economic status in the immediate post-World War II period, and there is little doubt that the new civil rights climate of the 1960's would have given the existing trends a boost. Since the native-born Hispanic population was then small, this means it probably could have achieved equality through integration relatively quickly. But the arrival of millions of immigrants who brought with them their Third World standards has made it increasingly difficult to close the socio-economic gap between the Hispanic and Anglo communities. Of course, as with African-Americans, many Hispanics have been successful in every way; but, again as with African-Americans, their number has not grown as rapidly as has that of those stuck at the bottom rungs in the agricultural and urban barrio communities. Add to this the increasingly entrenched language differences, and one can see why the prospects for full Hispanic integration into the broader society seem less optimistic than they did in the 1950's and 1960's.

Rivera is not unaware of the problems resulting from continued immigration. He knows that as more Mexican immigrants have arrived, the country has become both less willing and less able to absorb the Hispanic community into the main stream. But numbers also mean political power, and if it ultimately proves impossible to meld the Anglo and Hispanic communities into one equal society, then it will be numbers and power that determine the extent of the Hispanic territory that emerges.

In any case, Rivera says he knows that once Hispanics have achieved either an equal chance in a united America or the establishment of their own separate territory, they must turn their full attention to raising the socio-economic standards of the entire Hispanic community. And that, of course, means putting the brakes on immigration. But for the present, whatever his personal views, he knows that accepting continued immigration is a necessary bow to Hispanic political reality. Immigration could not soon be stopped without a fundamental enhancement of federal police and even military power along the border and in Hispanic areas, which Hispanics would consider an infringement on their civil rights and a blatant insult. Any federal clampdown on immigration now would obviously be aimed primarily at Hispanics, and they would take it as an implication that they were seen as somehow less worthy than other groups who arrived in the past without facing such restrictions. Many thoughtful Hispanics know this view is wrong -- that the U.S. plainly no longer needs immigrants as it did in the past. But to an Hispanic activist, already somewhat sensitive about racial and ethnic questions, any talk about an end to Hispanic immigration is likely to be taken as a slight.

Revolutions to the South

As economic decline and political revolution swept first through Central America, then certain countries of South America and Mexico, millions of people of all classes fled to the U.S. to escape the turmoil. With the struggles continuing and the populations of these already over-populated areas still growing rapidly, few people believe the refugee flow is likely to stop any time soon. It seems to be universally known, even to the poorest Latin American peasant, that the U.S. border is a sieve and that once one gets into the U.S., it is easy to claim to be a political refugee from "leftist" or "rightist" oppression. Furthermore, most have no doubt heard in a general way that in America, the process of expelling those who have a questionable claim to refugee status is so expensive and bothersome for the government that in the end only a token few are ever actually expelled.

The number of refugees from Mexico, where revolutionary leader Rafael Cardela is quite happy to encourage the exodus, has probably approached 6 million by now. That figure includes only refugees from the current revolution, and does not include the millions of earlier illegal immigrants. The number of recent refugees equals perhaps 4 percent of the Mexican population, and some people predict that the number will eventually exceed the 10 percent of the Cuban population which came to America after Castro. This could well be the case, as it is obviously a great deal easier to cross the poorly defended U.S.--Mexican border than it was for Cubans to cross the 90 miles of ocean separating them from Florida.

Cardela has good reasons for encouraging the exodus, as he knows that Mexico suffers from population pressure. Prior to his revolution, the population was growing annually by over two million, yet the country was barely able to provide three-quarters of a million new full-time jobs per year, even at bare subsistence wages. Except for the small middle and upper classes, standards had been going steadily down for some time, not only in regard to income but even more so in terms of the quality of life, as the pressures of crowding and the risks and discomforts of environmental deterioration made life increasingly less pleasant, particularly in the bloated urban areas. In respect to the middle and upper classes, Cardela, like Castro a half century earlier, realizes that their departure for the U.S. will have two fortunate spinoffs: it will reduce the size of the political opposition he faces, and increase the quantity of property he can confiscate "for the revolution." One may suspect also that he is quite pleased to contribute to America's problems of uncontrollable borders and ethnic disunity, just as Castro no doubt got much private pleasure from contemplating the problems he gave the U.S. when he let the Marielistas go in 1980.

Rivera's Long--Range Goal

I have already suggested the two possible outcomes Rivera sees for Hispanic America: integration on the basis of full equality or some form of separate status. In an ideal world he would prefer the former, with special status for Spanish as a second official language. Under such an arrangement, there would be integration and equality in the political and economic realms, but Hispanic culture and values would be preserved in the family and the community. It would be similar to the situation of certain well-integrated Asian-American communities, except that the scope and impact of Hispanic culture would occupy a much greater position in the American spectrum, reflecting the larger Hispanic population. In all probability, some such arrangement is what most other Hispanics would also choose in an ideal world.

However, because of existing and foreseeable demographic and socio-economic realities, Rivera sees this as increasingly unattainable. That being so, he is leaning toward what has been called the "Quebec solution." This implies that there would be a defined area, analogous to French-speaking Quebec Province in Canada, in which Spanish would be the official language, Hispanic culture would be dominant, and every legal means would be used to promote Hispanic interests, including economic ones.

With the Hispanic and Anglo populations and interests so thoroughly mixed in the southwestern border states today, working out a definable Quebec-type territory would not be easy. As Rivera remarked in a recent speech to an Hispanic audience, "The division, if it comes, should basically be along lines of population distribution at the time it is worked out with Anglo-America." This is one reason, of course, why he is willing to let Hispanic immigrants continue to pour in. The greater the Hispanic population becomes, the stronger its bargaining position will be if in the future it comes to defining a separate territory.

Whether in such a solution the lines would be drawn along existing state boundaries or along demographic lines which cut across the states is a question which, Rivera says, only time can decide. In states such as New Mexico, where the Hispanic population is evenly distributed, perhaps whole states would be involved. It would be very difficult, however, to convince, say, northern Californians, to accept Hispanic dominance, no matter how great a majority of Hispanic voters the entire state might then have.

A Quebec-type solution would still leave millions of Hispanics scattered throughout the rest of the country. Rivera sees no reason why establishing a predominantly Hispanic and Spanish-speaking region would require that all Hispanics from other areas migrate to it. They should be allowed to lead their daily lives in peace and prosperity elsewhere in America, just as Anglos should be allowed to do if they chose to remain in Hispanic territory. "The difference from today would be that Hispanics elsewhere would have new pride in the knowledge that their culture and language were officially recognized as equal. Furthermore, they would feel that they had a kind of safety valve -- a 'homeland' to which they could escape if ever life became uncomfortable in the Anglo-dominated world. They would be like French Canadians, who can be quite successful and happy in the English-speaking provinces, but who will always feel a special pride in and cultural closeness to Quebec."

PUBLISHER'S NOTE: The 2016 edition of this book contained a brief epilogue in which the author ventured certain speculations concerning the outcome of the approaching election and its implications for the United States. The author is now (2023) able to write an actual history of the post-election years, so he feels his earlier speculations have become moot; therefore, at his specific request, the first-edition epilogue has been omitted in this edition.

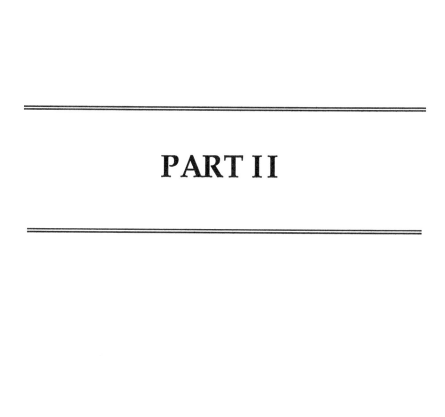

PART II

FOREWORD

I was pleased with the Indian reception of the 2016 edition of this work. And I was further gratified when the editors at Singh-Gandhi Publishing Co. informed me that the earlier edition could stand without change as Part I of this revised edition because, if I may confess, this saves me a good bit of work. I found it very easy to agree with their observation that retaining the original wording would not only facilitate early publication, but could help give readers a feel for how things stood back in 2016, on the verge of the historic transformation that is the subject of Part II.

Ravi Patel
Washington, D.C. and New Delhi
November 2023

CHAPTER FOUR

2016 TO 2020: THE SOUTH

In the election of November 2016, the American Freedom Party (AFP) candidate, Andrew Camp, won with over 55% of the vote. Once in office the following January, he did precisely what he had said during the campaign he intended to do: he declared a national emergency and took steps to institute martial law in every city in which rioting or urban guerrilla warfare had not been brought under control by the local authorities. This required formally federalizing the National Guard, including units already called to short-term duty by state governors; some regular Army units were also assigned.

Such actions would have been vigorously opposed just a year earlier, but by 2017 disorder was so widespread that no governor or mayor objected. Many mayors actively supported Camp while others, who would have lost local minority support if they had openly welcomed martial law, justified their lack of opposition by pointing out that it would have been futile. The truth was that even most of the black mayors strongly approved in private since they saw noother way to bring order to their cities. The immediate result of martial law was not order and calm, however. It was an escalation of guerrilla warfare to the point that no place in the large ghettoized cities was safe. Every citizen could find him- or herself in a battle zone at any time.

The ghetto radicals quickly realized they could turn to their advantage the fact that, as they told their communities, "now there is no escape." Since you can't stay safely on the sidelines, they said, you might as well join us. Some ghetto residents who had until then considered themselves moderates agreed, and for the first time committed themselves to the rebels. As one formerly fence-straddling black leader told this reporter: "Andrew Camp's fascist oppression has removed any lingering hope of ever seeing a peaceful and just resolution to the problem of ghettoized black cities in a white America. What the radicals have been saying is right. The old racist system cannot be reformed; it must be destroyed."

The side of the rebels was also strengthened by the adherence of a certain number of former drug dealers and people who had spent time in prison. These elements -- often people of considerable talent

-- had in many cases sunk into crime out of hopelessness and alienation from the existing society. To them, the society had seemed to offer no alternatives between utterly dead end jobs at below subsistence wages, and the search for a modicum of excitement, status and "good living" through crime. But now a few began to listen as polished political agitators told them their criminal behavior had been the result of an unjust racist system which had given them no choice. The African-American community, they were told, now needed their energies for the struggle, and actively encouraged them to respond positively to this opportunity to solve the community's problems. The agitators argued that now, for the first time, the opportunity existed to deal a fatal blow to the oppressive system. Many who had done time in jail were moved by the chance to strike back, and to feel themselves recognized as now behaving in an approved manner. With armed chaos spreading in almost every major northern city, King Dillon was garnering growing support from black leaders and intellectuals for his "Southern strategy," and there was also increasing talk about it, mostly favorable, down on the ghetto streets. Yet most people were understandably less than eager to uproot their lives and move south simply because they saw no immediate solution to ghetto problems or liked what they had seen of Dillon on TV. It would take more than earnest words to get people to abandon their homes, no matter how undesirable those homes might seem. Therefore Dillon decided to make a dramatic move, in order to spur the desired migration. In a critical speech in April 2017 in Gary, Indiana, he announced he was going to "put everything on the line." He would move his headquarters to Mississippi, taking with him his recently established bodyguard of over 2,000 men -- the Black Guards.

The Guards were a de facto personal army which seemed to some observers not unlike Mussolini's Blackshirts or Hitler's Storm Troopers of the last century. Such comparisons naturally made Dillon livid. His defenders argued that he had no choice but to establish a bodyguard, as he had become a very obvious target for white extremists and had received many death threats. They pointed out that, in the 1960's, the African-American community had not sufficiently protected its leaders, Dr. Martin Luther King, Jr., and Malcolm X, and that both had been gunned down. It was a mistake that the community had committed, and in the words of one activist: "Never again." Whether this necessitated a small army with distinctive uniforms bearing black-power symbols is another question. In any case, the Guards were well-trained and disciplined, many having had military training and experience due to the Persian Gulf wars and what Dillon liked to call "the undeclared bush wars conducted worldwide by administrations over the past several decades," and they ultimately played an important role as the nucleus of the militia force which defended the revolution in 2020.

In the Gary speech, Dillon emphasized that in the move south, the Guards would seek no violence and their weapons would be kept under wraps unless he or his caravan were attacked. Anticipating opposition from whites, particularly Mississippi whites, Dillon defended the move as completely legal: "There is no law prohibiting me or anyone else from moving across state lines to establish a new residence. We have a perfect right, as American citizens, to move south and to defend ourselves if attacked, and we will exercise that right."

In explaining to his fellow African-Americans why he felt the time was ripe for the move, Dillon reiterated the point made in his Congressional resignation speech of 2016 -- namely, that the higher black birth rate in the South had already pushed the black proportion of the population close to 50 percent; by early 2017, he asserted, Mississippi had become 46 percent black, South Carolina 42 percent and Louisiana 39 percent. The percentages for Alabama and Georgia were only slightly lower. Given these figures, he reasoned, a swift mass migration on top of the modest trickle that had followed the first public mention of the "Southern strategy" 10 months earlier could certainly push the three leading states, and possibly all five, toward black majorities by 2020. He claimed that millions of African-Americans had come to agree with him that the only way to solve the racial problem once and for all was for blacks to gain control over their own destinies, and that this meant for them to possess what all other "distinct national groups" demanded -- a homeland. For African-Americans, this could only be in the South, as they had no roots elsewhere. How many blacks actually agreed with him at this time on the need for a homeland cannot be known, but his casual reference to "millions" was probably correct. The idea had simmered in the African-American communities in one form or another, through Garveyism and Pan-Africanism, the Nation of Islam and the Republic of New Afrika movement, for a century. He had plainly stirred a lot of minds once again -- regardless of how small the actual number of migrants.

Further, he expressed confidence that a large and sudden influx of blacks following a determined leadership -- implying, of course, himself -- would be able to overcome any opposition from whites. He concluded with an impassioned call for an exodus from the ghettoes to follow him in "building a new destiny for black America." But he did caution that there should be no misunderstanding about one thing: times would be very tough for years to come, and anyone not prepared for a lengthy struggle had better stay put.

The day after the Gary speech, Dillon and the Black Guards left Chicago in a long caravan of cars and trucks, and drove straight south. As they passed through towns en route, they got some curious stares but there were no hostile incidents until they reached the Mississippi border the following day. There they were met by white vigilantes and a contingent of state troopers who blocked the way. Tension filled the air. The state troopers realized they were vastly outnumbered by Dillon's caravan plus several thousand Mississippi blacks who had come to meet them at the border. After some strong words including the arguments of lawyers accompanying Dillon on the unassailable legality of their actions and the likely ramifications of their being turned back by force in full sight of the national media which had converged to capture the historic moment, the state troopers cleared the vigilantes from the road without any shots being fired, and let the vehicles pass. The caravan went directly to a large farm in the east-central part of the state which had been purchased by Dillon's agents.

The ghetto response to his move south was just what Dillon had hoped for. Enormous enthusiasm swept the streets. The hodge-podge jargon of revolution which was commonplace on ghetto streets, on circulated tapes of suppressed black vocalists, on the limited wattage radio broadcasts of local black stations, and among street-side agitators, became liberally salted with concepts from Dillon's speeches. From cab drivers to housewives to drug dealers, in addition to talk of "revolution" or "liberation" or "overturning four centuries of oppression," the phrases "having our own land and a government of our own" and "controlling our own political destinies" were on every lip.

The ghettoes by this time had become truly desperate in terms of food and, increasingly, other necessities. The welfare system had broken down entirely, as first white taxpayers and then white-dominated legislatures had resolved to stop "throwing money" at the problems of the ghettoes. To whites the billions spent every year in living memory had seemed to make nary a dent in the ghetto condition. The result of the anti-welfare crusade was that masses of ghettoites who had known no income except welfare were thrown onto the streets to join the masses of black homeless, for whom the welfare safety net had long ago disappeared. Such people, terrified of meeting the fate of the homeless, many of whom had succumbed to physical and mental disease, were prepared to grasp at any straw by the time they heard Dillon's call for a black homeland. Within days of Dillon's speech, the existing trickle of migration had turned into a steady flow. People headed south in cars, trains, buses and, from the middle states, even on bicycle and on foot. Although Dillon and his aides urged migrants to pay for their needs and to obey all laws as they trekked south, many of the migrants had no money, while those used to seizing or inveigling the wherewithal to meet their needs behaved as they always had. There were, consequently, some incidents of theft and violence as certain among the migrants resorted to taking whatever they needed whenever they needed it. There would have been more such incidents had it not been for the fact that many whites in the northern cities were happy to see the ghetto populations depart, and helped them with generous gifts of food and money, in some cases even with transportation. Thousands were given free bus and train tickets.

Within four months, by August 2017, over 1.5 million blacks from the North and West had made their way to the South. It was a population movement not unlike that of Hindus and Muslims following the creation of Pakistan, though on a smaller scale, and much more peaceful. The greatest number went at first to Mississippi, simply because that was where Dillon was based and where they knew a black majority had been achieved shortly after his arrival. But Dillon was eager to spread the arriving migrants through the other states also, so he set up an office to help settle them in housing and jobs throughout the five states. Where no jobs could be found, the migrants were sent to help establish communal farms -- based on the "commune" which had been developed on the farm which now served as Dillon's headquarters.

The commune scheme was one of the more innovative -- not to mention, unlikely -- developments in the early days of the black-dominated South. Back in late 2015, when Dillon's people had purchased the 4,000 acre headquarters farm (later expanded to 9,000 acres with the purchase of adjoining land), they hadn't given much thought to what they wanted to do with the land itself. The farm was seen simply as a kind of beachhead in the South, a safe base from which Dillon's representatives could operate. They knew, of course, that its presence would not be greeted with joy by neighboring white farmers and that it might be subject to threats, so from the beginning it was patrolled by well-armed guards. But as for how the land might be put to use by these guards and other migrants (including some local folk who wandered in and whose recent history of relations with the law was not probed too deeply), there was no plan until one of Dillon's on-the-spot advisers suggested they might as well attempt to farm it. Some local black farmers were brought in to show them how to do it, and by the time Dillon arrived in 2017 the experiment was proceeding smoothly, with the commune supplying a good portion of its own needs as well as selling produce to nearby black town dwellers.

Ultimately this first commune played a valuable role as a model for others, and many of its residents became mentors as new communes were set up. The commune-model role was, however, always supplementary to the farm's main function. With Dillon coordinating the migration from it, the farm came to be seen by many blacks as a kind of alternative seat of government -- and it continued to be seen as such, and in many ways to operate as such, right up to the events of 2020.

Even after seeing the success of the headquarters farm, most observers considered it a special case and saw the idea of using it as the model for a South-wide commune movement as less than inspired. They said nothing could be more hopeless than turning street-wise ghettoites into farmers. But Dillon knew that once the migration got going in earnest, there would be large numbers of people who would find no jobs in the South. So, after his interest had been piqued by a Chinese visitor's reference to Mao-era communes in that country, he read up on China's experience (which left him cold) and that of the Israelis in Palestine after World War II. The latter made a strong impression, particularly the accounts of how people from the "ghettoes" of Eastern Europe had been settled in the communal "kibbutzim" and immediately put to useful and productive work, despite their lack of agricultural experience. In such communes, people could grow their own food and produce other basic needs, while anything above bare subsistence would depend on their own initiative. In short, they wouldn't starve, and if they were willing to work hard they could become reasonably prosperous.

Dillon was not so naive as to believe that urban blacks would adjust to rural communal life with ease, but he could think of no better plan for settling those with no job skills. The only alternative that anyone could offer was a massive, government-funded public works program, which Dillon's camp was already seeking from the federal government, in the name of reparations for "300 years of slavery," insisting that their case was equally as deserving of consideration as that of the Japanese who had been interned during World War II, and whose reparation claims had been settled in the 1980's. In this, they drew support from a number of groups which had united in this effort over the past several decades. This, however, was still regarded as an objective that could not be gained in the short term.

The immediate problem was how to acquire the needed land. At first, Dillon's representatives simply bought what they could, but the quantity of decent land available at moderate cost was small. With blacks pouring in by the thousands each day, Dillon knew it would not be long before the land question became critical -- and he realized he could not avoid an early confrontation with white landowners on the issue.

He began publicly to encourage African-Americans to settle as squatters on farmable land that was not being used, proclaiming that as land was "a gift from God," it was not right that some should have more than they could use while others would starve for lack of it. Others justified their seizure on the basis of the century-and-a half old promise of "40 acres and a mule." White farmers protested this "unconstitutional theft of land," and there was some talk of resisting it by force. But the reality was that an increasing number of whites hoped to avoid a full-scale confrontation with Dillon's movement and were willing to make concessions where necessary -- provided black demands didn't go too far. As one influential white farm leader explained it to me: "With the black population growing rapidly, thoughtful southern whites are aware they will have to make adjustments to lead tolerable lives in a black-majority South. They resist the thought of fleeing the South in panic, losing the property accumulated over a lifetime, and the corollary of this is they will have to learn to live with King Dillon." For the moment, this approach meant tolerating certain unpleasant demands and pressures, such as squatters on surplus land, provided it meant no direct threat to the whites' own livelihood. Of course, not all whites were so willing to sit back and passively accept evolutionary change. Many were very angry, and private talk of using force to halt Dillon was becoming more common. Few doubted that such talk would eventually lead to action.

As for the new black migrants, themselves, squatting on bits of surplus white land was still a long way from a solution to the land problem, as white farmers still occupied and utilized most of the best land. If blacks were to achieve the solid agricultural base that Dillon had indicated was an essential part of a genuine "homeland," they would need to acquire a substantial -- and ultimately a roughly proportional -- share of this prime land. Fortunately for Dillon, the number of whites who were beginning to see their future in the South as hopeless (insofar as it concerned living in an African-American dominated territory, with all the changes that that would mean in terms of culture and past privileges) was, though still small, on the rise. And they were willing to sell their land for quite a bit less than they would have considered its fair market value just months earlier. This was especially true in Mississippi, of course, which was on the cutting edge of change all through 2017 and 2018.

Dillon was happy to see these whites leave, both because that made more land available for establishing communes, and because he wanted as soon as possible to realize solid African-American majorities throughout the first states, and thus give African-Americans the advantages of access to state funds, planning and programming. The issue was delicate, however, and Dillon always felt that it would not be in the black interest to have a general exodus of whites. Not only were white skills and capital needed to assure a prosperous South, but also, the existence of a white minority in the black South would help keep pressure on the North to give fair treatment to African-Americans who remained there. Nevertheless, as of 2017 and 2018, with blacks not yet in commanding majorities, a modest white outflow was still something to be encouraged.

In a June 2018 television forum on the future of the South, Dillon remarked that whites would be welcomed and "could prosper in the future African-American majority South in a way most blacks had never prospered in the white-ruled South." Nevertheless, since the distribution of wealth and property in the South was grossly uneven, a future government dedicated to equal opportunity for all "would have no choice but to work toward altering the distribution of wealth-producing property in significant ways." Otherwise the wealth and privileges of the existing propertied class, mostly white of course, would be so entrenched that African-Americans would remain "a permanently poor lower class in their own land." Therefore, in regard to the land question, although white farmers could count on retaining their homes and "enough land for a family to farm," the new black-dominated governments should "take active measures to achieve a more equal distribution of land." He then brought up a proposal for a property tax with a progressive rate structure designed to tax small individual holdings of land or holdings of small appraised value at a low rate while taxing larger and more highly valued holdings at progressively higher rates. The rates at the upper end would be set high enough to encourage those with large quantities of unused or underused land to sell it to the state, which would then re-sell it to small private farmers or allocate it for commune use. At the same time, Dillon went on, there should be a steeply progressive state income tax with rates on the richest set high enough to generate the revenues needed for "all essential state purposes" -- including the purchase of land, equal and high-quality education for all, public housing and law enforcement. In short, the plan was to squeeze some of the excess land and wealth out of the rich (mainly whites) for the benefit of the non-rich (mainly blacks).

In response to a question from the audience as to whether his proposed land policies couldn't be considered "state robbery of land," Dillon contended that whites had originally stolen the land from the Indians and had made it productive and valuable on the backs of black slave labor. Achieving a more equal distribution of land, therefore, was in part simply a righting of historical wrongs. "The only moral course in regard to the God-given resource of land," he said, "is to make sure that all who need it have access to a fair share. We intend to do this."

Another forum participant offered the thought that the Supreme Court might find the proposed policies unconstitutional. No doubt feeling on the defensive, Dillon, who rarely allowed himself to be goaded into making remarks he later regretted, countered with the unfortunate response, "To hell with the Supreme Court; we're talking here about justice and equality. Once our state governments are in full control, there will be little the White House, the Pentagon or the Supreme Court can legally do to prevent the fair distribution of land or any other measures needed to achieve equality for African-Americans." He went on to observe that after World War II, the U.S. had advocated the redistribution of land in several countries and had carried it out during the occupation of Japan, where former land owners were given compensation well below market value for their confiscated land. Therefore, he concluded, "I don't see how anyone can criticize this part of our program as being un-American. It's something we've been encouraging South American governments to undertake for their own good for years."

The reaction of whites to Dillon's proposed tax scheme was not long in coming. Outrage was widespread, new vigilante groups were formed, and an unambiguously-named White Citizens Land Council (WCLC) headquartered in Atlanta with branches throughout the South was established, with the explicit purpose of preparing to "defend against any illegal attempt to take white land or property." WCLC leaders made no attempt to hide the fact that they were inclined to respond with force not only to land seizure, but to anything they saw as a threat to the existing political and economic system in the South. There is no doubt that the WCLCs had active Ku Klux Klan (KKK) participation, but the leaders tried to play this down in public. They still hoped to maintain a veneer of legality about their resistance to the black takeover. That is, they weren't planning to initiate random and "unjustified" violence against blacks, but were only resisting the illegal black takeover of land, "unconstitutional" and "confiscatory" tax schemes, and alleged "loading up of electoral districts with transient migrants for the sole purpose of swinging elections."

As for the KKK, by 2017 it had generally become recognized even among whites as an extremist fringe, and public support for it was so small that it could generally be ignored in political discourse. However, Klan leaders were always ready to use age-old violent methods employed ever since post-Civil War Reconstruction days, and everyone knew that a racial showdown in the South would bring the Klan out of the shadows. Furthermore, the active, public Klan was small compared to the element which fully sympathized with it and occasionally contributed money, but could not risk public affiliation. From 2017 on, these backdoor supporters spent a lot of time in angry discussion about unfolding events, and managed to slip a growing quantity of funds into the hands of the activists.

Ever since the emergence of the mediagenic David Duke into statewide Louisiana politics in 1990, there had also been a "presentable," ostensibly mainstream group of politicians who publicly denied any connection to the KKK, but which everyone assumed to have close behind-the-scenes ties. These immaculately-dressed and articulate politicians had many local successes and won a few Congressional seats, but were generally shunned or dealt with perfunctorily by those northern and southern politicians whose political lives depended on appealing to a wider multi-ethnic constituency. With Dillon's increasing talk of radical policies to shake the foundations of southern inequality, it didn't take great insight to see that the Klan would eventually be heard from again.

Shortly after the above-mentioned television forum, the WCLC leader in Jackson, Mississippi had managed to persuade a number of his state's branch leaders, and even the commander of a U.S. Army infantry division stationed in the state, that Dillon's radical egalitarian talk represented nothing less than a "socialistic threat to the American way of life in the South." The general, however, was not eager to be catapulted into action that might meet with Washington's disapproval, so he sought permission from the Pentagon before making any move against Dillon's farm base. The answer from the Pentagon -- which at the time had its hands more than full in helping to control the on-going disruption in cities throughout the North -- was slow in coming and ambiguous when it came. The general chose to interpret its references to "protecting constitutional government" and "instituting martial law even in rural areas where justified," as sufficiently sweep-ing to cover an attack on Dillon's headquarters.

The assault force consisted of two infantry battalions accompa-nied by some 300 WCLC vigilantes who had been hastily sworn in as sheriff's deputies. The latter were supposed to make the necessary arrests and searches while the soldiers occupied the base and main-tained security. The raid began at dawn on a foggy October (2018) morning and the troops immediately ran into sniper fire from the woods; the Black Guards, it turned out, had not at all been taken by surprise. The inexperienced and ill-prepared attack force was turned back within an hour, to the shock of the general, who later admitted he had been expecting to walk in unopposed to accept a quick surrender. Four soldiers were killed and 15 wounded in the action; no casualties were reported among the Black Guards.

This abortive attempt to eliminate Dillon's base was the closest thing to open warfare in the South up to the events of 2020, although relatively minor violence between armed blacks and white vigilantes had occurred prior to Dillon's arrival and continued to occur sporadically. The nation's and the world's TV screens were of course filled with U.S. interracial incidents during this period, but it was primarily scenes from the northern cities, where urban guerrilla warfare was on-going, despite martial law.

In the aftermath of the attack on the farm base, some of Dillon's supporters urged taking revenge on nearby white residents known to be connected with the WCLCs, but Dillon urged restraint, feeling that if black-white tensions exploded at that time, blacks could only be the losers. They did not yet have the numbers or the power to face a fully aroused white population which felt its back was to the wall. So his press secretary let it be known that at a meeting with his colleagues a few days after the attack, he had again stressed his view that whites willing to cooperate on a basis of fairness and equality must be allowed to feel secure in the South. The best hope for a non-disruptive transition to a prosperous black-majority South still lay in retaining the skills of cooperative, non-racist whites, he said.

In further attempting to defuse tensions in the following months, Dillon repeatedly leaned toward the side of moderation, holding a series of meetings with white representatives designed, as he put it, "to avert misunderstandings that could spark another unfortunate armed incident." The most important result of these was an arrangement for cooperation between existing local authorities and the so-called Neighborhood Protective Associations (NPAs) in patrolling the African-American communities of the South. The NPAs were a combination of neighborhood watch groups and auxiliary black militia which the Black Guards were busily setting up in urban black communities throughout the five states.

This black-white cooperative law enforcement effort was promoted by Dillon in part to calm white fears about the further spread of urban chaos, which so far had not been as bad as in the North. Equally important, however, was his awareness that a successful black-governed South could not be achieved unless crime and drugs in the ghettoes were suppressed. And black-white law enforcement cooperation was plainly essential in achieving this.

In explaining to African-American radicals why they now had to work more closely with white authorities in policing the ghettoes, Dillon engaged in some plain speaking about black crime. He noted that too many blacks, having felt themselves to be part of a scorned minority, were accustomed to explaining the high black crime rate as an understandable (though not, of course, commendable) response to victimization by inequality and injustice. That attitude had to change. With African-Americans about to assume meaningful political responsibility in a significant territory they must, said Dillon, learn that cooperating with legitimate governmental authorities, black or white, could no longer be viewed as "selling out to the enemy." His push for racial cooperation in maintaining law and order won a favorable response from most members of the black community. The NPA, in quiet but effective cooperation with some officially trained black police, devoted themselves to problems within predominantly African-American communities, leaving white police to handle white communities. In the past, black police in some communities had been seen as puppets of the official white establishment. Now, with the local black police and the NPA assuming major responsibility for order in the African-American communities, the former tension between the communities and the police was greatly reduced. Law and order was not something that could be achieved overnight, but thanks to vigorous NPA and police action plus active community support, street crime began before long to be reduced in southern cities.

One major problem facing law enforcement was the vast number of guns in the ghetto -- as well as throughout the society. Creating safe streets was impossible where every lunatic, misfit or crook had access to a gun, including in many cases, automatics. Therefore, in the years that followed these first law-and-order moves, as each new black-majority state government began to function, Dillon's people insisted that laws prohibiting privately owned handguns and auto-matic weapons be passed and strictly enforced. They nevertheless provided for citizen militias well-equipped with small arms of genuine military use. (These state militias, which grew out of the Black Guards, played an important role in 2020, and Dillon says they will continue to exist for as long as there remains even a remote possibility of an attempt by the white government in the North to reverse the course being taken in the South. The first abortive raid on the "Farm" had turned out to be a blessing in disguise, as it convinced any doubters of the value of a separate black militia.)

A critical step in achieving an orderly society was to end the drug culture. For generations, large numbers of ghetto blacks had been attempting to escape the frustrations of the ghetto by getting spaced out on drugs, and Dillon knew it would be no easy task to end such a deeply entrenched subculture. Yet to Dillon the task seemed far from impossible. "Look at Havana under Batista," Dillon argued privately, "and the opium dens in China before the revolution.   A society can control drugs when it has the moral and political will and when it offers its people a change in conditions." He saw the task as absolutely essential, because a self-respecting black society could not tolerate massive drug abuse. It is not known just what instruc-tions Dillon gave his drug enforcers, but there is some evidence that in those early days, the NPAs simply rounded up known drug dealers and disposed of them. In any case, drugs rather quickly began to become scarce. The problem did not disappear entirely, however. When the rewards are high enough, someone can always be found who is willing to take the risk of smuggling or distributing drugs -- and as scarcity drove drug prices up, the rewards became substantial indeed. But the squeeze was definitely on, and drug use steadily dropped. This was certainly due not only to direct efforts at drug suppression, but also in no small part to the rebirth of hope among formerly hopeless and disaffected black youth as the vision of a black rebirth in the South spread among them.

The newly-elected African-American state governments con-tinue today to be very tough in dealing with drugs. Legally convicted drug dealers are executed, and drug users -- as well as other trouble-makers -- are hauled off to do compulsory labor either on communes or on public projects such as road-building or park maintenance.

Dillon has long believed in the efficacy of reform-through-labor programs, which he had learned about during a visit to Azania in 2014.

The November 2018 Election: Black Majorities in Four States

The period between Dillon's move south in early 2017 and the Congressional election of 2018 was critical in changing the demographic shape of the South. At the beginning of 2017, no state had a black majority, but by November 2018 there were African-American majorities in Mississippi, South Carolina, Alabama and Louisiana, with the black population of Georgia just short of a majority.

This period was also the critical one in solidifying the communes. By late 2018 there were several communes in each state and a substantial body of experience had been built up. New arrivals with no other prospects could be settled quickly and with confidence that however tough their new lives might be, the people in charge knew what they were doing and would assure tolerable working and living conditions.

One surprising development was that as soon as communal workers gained a bit of farming experience, they were eager to demonstrate their initiative on private plots, so the land of the communes began to be divided into main-crop fields worked communally by teams and smaller vegetable plots worked by individuals and families. This was an arrangement not dissimilar to that adopted in several Asian socialist countries late in the 20th Century. The communes were important psychologically as evidence that formerly hopeless and skill-less African-Americans could effectively function in a productive economic venture. Critics who had originally seen the communes as nothing more than a last-resort dumping ground for black migrants with nowhere else to go were pleasantly surprised to see them become a significant and positive factor in the black movement. Despite their importance, however, the number of people who joined them never exceeded a small percentage of the black population. As had long been the case, the majority of all blacks in the South, including the new migrants, lived in cities and towns.

As the communes grew in this early period, some blacks in each state participated in what amounted to an informal boycott of the white farm economy. That is, wherever possible, they bought what they needed from the communes or private African-American farmers. This led to something of a dual farm economy in the South: on the one hand a black one composed of existing private farms plus the communes, and on the other, a white one which continued to be the major supplier of supermarket chains. The former, though poor, was growing, while the latter was distinctly suffering, though by no means near collapse. White customers shopped in the white-run stores as always, and blacks also patronized them for the many products not available from the communes or in black-run stores.

In the election of 2018 an unprecedented 80 percent of eligible African-Americans and 85 percent of eligible whites voted in the South, with the vote going almost entirely along racial lines. In three states, black majorities were elected in the legislatures, and black candidates also won in the two states which had gubernatorial elections. It was clear to all that blacks would have the numbers to control the legislatures of all five states by 2020.

The African-Americans elected in 2018 were with almost no exceptions vigorously committed to Dillon's program for using the power of black majority governments to push toward economic equality. That is, they favored using the taxing power to fund the effort to expand the public sector's ability to eliminate the causes of black inferiority by providing all citizens equal and high quality education, safe streets, adequate medical care and, where necessary, jobs or job training, whether on the communes or elsewhere. These programs would be expensive, and Dillon's backers did not shy from straightforward talk about well-off voters having to learn to live not only with highly progressive state income and property taxes, but also with a higher sales tax than in the past on so-called "vice" items such as tobacco and alcohol, and on most items not classified as basic necessities. Although Dillon did not talk explicitly of "socialism," neither did he react negatively when others described his program as "socialistic."

When Dillon's backers raised these proposals in state legislatures, there was an eruption of anger and hot words. Most white legislators bitterly opposed such ideas and made their opposition abundantly clear. However, they knew where to draw the line in confronting the black contingents. On the few occasions where they allowed overt racism to creep into their words, black legislators knew they had won moral victories. Such talk had long since become unacceptable in governing bodies, and to use it was a sign of desperation -- of "losing your cool." The great majority of whites hoped for continued social order and rule of law -- knowing that if it broke down they would be the biggest immediate sufferers -- so they tried to "bring black legislators to their senses" through the art of persuasion. Dillon's backers, however, now had a program that gave them a kind of hope they had not previously known, and they were not to be talked out of it. The generally civil, though far from friendly, atmosphere in the state legislatures persisted until November 2020.

A significant factor in Dillon's favor was that whereas the black community was almost 100 percent behind him, the white community in the South was becoming increasingly split. Some hoped to use force to halt the Dillon-led black takeover, and they backed the more extreme WCLC vigilante groups, which still dreamed of driving the black migrants back north. Others, knowing the past could not be reborn, hoped to remain as a relatively prosperous and free minority, not unlike the Afrikaners who remained in Azania. But growing numbers lived in daily doubt about the future, and were desperately trying to decide whether they should sell their homes and land for whatever they could get and leave the South.

As reluctant as white extremists were to admit it, the flow from the northern cities could not be reversed. In fact, the migration was now emptying the ghettoes to such an extent that for the first time, the police and military forces in some northern cities were able to regain full control.

The middle-class, integrated minority of blacks in the North had not been as quick as the victims of poverty to respond to Dillon's vision of an alternative political destiny. But as they began to be swept up in the tide of black nationalism flowing out from the South, they realized that they, no less than white Southerners, faced a difficult choice: should they remain as a small and prosperous but powerless minority in the North, or should they head south and participate in what was probably the only hope for blacks to determine their own future as a nationality. In the end, those inclined to view the world in terms of political aspirations headed south, while those who were primarily interested in enjoying the material comforts for which they had spent their lives striving stayed in the North, even after 2020.

2020: *The Move Toward Separatism*

As a result of black immigration and the white exodus, by early 2020 all five states of the new South had African-American majorities, ranging from about 70 percent in Mississippi to 55 percent in Georgia. The figures are not known precisely since everything was in such a state of flux at the time that no effective census could be taken in the South during that census year. In any case, no one could doubt that blacks would sweep the November elections. Dillon himself did not run for any formal office, but almost all African-American candidates in the region ran as his dedicated followers. Shortly before the election, Dillon told a reporter that he saw himself as being in a position "somewhat like that of Mahatma Gandhi -- though not quite so convinced that non-violence will work." He was, of course, alluding to the fact that the famous 20th Century pacifist was generally recognized as the leader of the Indian independence struggle, though he had no formal high office.

President Andrew Camp was renominated by the AFP in July, and built his campaign around a call both to finish the task of bringing order to the ghettoes and to suppress what he now called the "communist rebellion" in the South. Some observers saw this rhetorical flourish as a throwback to the post-World War II McCarthy era, but the existence of the communes and Dillon's regular praise for their admittedly communalistic ideals made many voters accept the "communist" label. Camp also explicitly accused Dillon of planning to split the nation apart, adding in one speech: "We fought a war to stop the Confederate secessionists of the 1860's, and if necessary we'll fight to stop the communist secessionists now." While holding out the threat of military force as the ultimate "stick," he left no doubt that he had also taken other steps to stop Dillon. He had "directed the FBI and every other security agency of the Federal Government to investigate and use whatever means are necessary to put an end to this conspiracy of Mr. Dillon and his rebel band to destroy our national unity." The lack of specificity on Camp's part concerning "whatever means are necessary" was no doubt meant to bring home to Dillon the government's willingness to resort to covert action, as well as legal means, to stop him.

In branding Dillon not only a communist but a secessionist, Camp was leaping to a conclusion beyond anything Dillon had stated publicly -- or, as far as I know, even privately. But plainly the question of what political form the black South should ultimately take was very much on his mind. On the one hand, he had for some time been quite willing to admit in private conversation that his "loyalty to the United States {was} minimal to non-existent," having been fully supplanted by his loyalty and commitment to a black "homeland" in the South. He explained that this was the only reasonable position he could take since the Camp-dominated United States Government was "dedicated to preserving the status quo" -- which meant the continued inequality and ghetto-confinement of blacks. On the other hand, he was more than a little reluctant to cut the cord with the North, as he felt there were distinct advantages to free contacts and close cooperation with the rest of the nation insofar as they did not interfere with the establishment of an economically-viable, black-run political entity in the South.

Based on a talk I had with Dillon in mid-2020 -- the last such conversation before the crisis later that year -- he still favored nothing more than some sort of autonomous status for the South. The black-majority southern states should remain part of the United States, he said, but there would have to be some new guidelines for the federal union, with the South enjoying greater independence than did the states under the old system. He relished the irony when he emphasized "the need for more attention to state's rights and less interference from Washington." The states of the new black South, he elaborated, must have greater freedom to tax, and be able to control immigration and operate militias within their own borders. He even talked of a separate regional court system which could not be overruled by the Supreme Court in Washington. I doubt, however, if he had given the latter suggestion a lot of in-depth analysis; more likely, it was a reflection of the fears he then had that the U.S. Supreme Court might soon try to strike down some of the laws passed in the black-governed states since 2018. As it was, the courts were clogged with suits lodged against Dillon, the communes, and the new state governments but no major cases had yet reached the Supreme Court.

Turning toward the future of economic relations between the South and the rest of the nation, Dillon said there would have to be a certain period of protection for newly-founded black industries, but eventually he would like to see the resumption of completely free economic relations between the regions. He also wanted the South to have the freedom to regulate its conduct of international trade, particularly with African nations, with the possibility of some use of barter to overcome problems resulting from the devastation of the currencies and credit of the Third World . At the conclusion of the interview, he admitted some doubts as to the long-term workability of the North-South relationship he was suggesting. But he observed optimistically that his ideas for a new federalism were not totally unlike the arrangements successfully worked out between China and Taiwan and the two Koreas in the decade since 2010.

As President Camp campaigned before the TV cameras in the months prior to the election, increasingly heavy hints issued from his lips indicating that the military option was being given strong consideration. This came as no surprise to Dillon, who by August had expressed concern that Camp was itching for a justification to settle the southern situation by force -- for the simple reason that there was no other way to settle it to his satisfaction. Consequently, at the same time Dillon's inner circle of advisers was trying to divine the future from the words emanating from the White House, his men in the communes were stepping up combat training for the black militias.

Distressed by the growing white exodus from the South, President Camp in late August went on TV to urge whites to remain there and assured them that the federal government would protect their rights. Whites would be needed to rebuild the South "once order has been re-established there," he added.

As Summer 2020 turned to Fall, additional signs reached Dillon and his inner circle indicating that Camp had ordered the Pentagon to draw up contingency plans for a military move after the November election. In fact, Dillon later informed me that in early October, he was told as much by a low-level Pentagon officer who was sympathetic to the black movement in the South. The officer also said Camp was under enormous pressure from within the government to use covert action, if necessary, to get rid of Dillon before it came to a military confrontation. (To date, it has not been possible for this writer to verify what, if any, covert actions might have been employed against Dillon.) It was well known, of course, that the FBI and the Secret Service had been keeping a close watch on Dillon ever since his break with Congress, while the CIA had spent an enormous amount of money trying to locate constantly rumored but, as far as this writer knows, never found ties between Dillon and foreign radical or terrorist groups. Despite the lack of known ties to such groups, it is widely assumed that Dillon's people have had informal contacts with representatives of anti-western governments abroad.

Upon hearing directly from his Pentagon contact that Camp was leaning closer to the military option, Dillon summoned the African-American leaders of the five states to meet at the "Farm" to discuss the situation. During four intense days of talks, all the options were weighed. There was general agreement that Camp had talked himself into a position from which it would be difficult to do nothing. He had to make some move, and neither Dillon nor any of the other participants doubted that the only real cards Camp could play were military. This being so, they agreed on the need to further expand the militia and intensify training, and to do it in a very public way that would make it clear that any military move would be very costly to the North. Also, Dillon would at the earliest opportunity give a speech brimming with firm resolve that the new African-American leadership of the South would never surrender to outside pressure.

In the words of this speech, delivered the day after the conference, Dillon said, "I speak for the people of the South in saying, no matter what the immediate outcome of Mr. Camp's schemes, we will not in the end be defeated, because the majority of the people of the South are firmly behind us." Appealing to the "good sense of the people of the North," he added: "We would like to have friendly, cooperative relations with Washington, but if Mr. Camp does what he seems to be saying he will do, such relations will be impossible. The moment his troops cross our borders or come out of their southern bases with aggressive intent, that will be the end of any hope for a normal and friendly federal relationship between North and South."

That was the public warning given in Dillon's speech, and it left no doubt that a military attack would help push the South toward separatism. But the decisions made in secret at the October "Farm" meeting went further, as it was later revealed. The black leaders decided that if Camp attacked, they would immediately issue a statement on the establishment of a separate regional government for the southern states, on the grounds that Camp's military aggression would make it impossible for the black South to continue to recognize the legitimacy of the government in Washington.

With the final wording of the statement agreed upon ahead of time, Dillon was able to read it to the press just hours after the northern forces began their assault early on November 10, one week after Camp's re-election. It declared in part:

> Andrew Camp and his government will not allow the will of the majority in the South to be realized. He is determined to crush democracy by force rather than allow democracy to bring about black power. This attitude is most unfortunate. We, the representatives of the new South, have always felt that we and the North would be better off in the years to come if the North had a white government which welcomed the African-American South as an equal partner. We could face the outside world together, study the same history, honor the same pioneers, both white and black, and trade and travel freely across borders. We would be one nation, but a truly federal one in which separate states and regions controlled their internal affairs as the majorities within those regions determined.

But Camp makes this impossible. He knows only force and oppression. And, let it be added, racism. He will send his hired FBI and CIA dirty tricks artists and assassins after us, and if they don't succeed, he will try to defeat us militarily. He has forced us to make a difficult choice. Are we to be part of a society which despises us, whose only answer to African-American majority rule dedicated to equality for all is to suppress it by force? Or do we pursue the only alternative, which is to go our own independent way, whatever the cost? Our pride, our honor, our simple self-respect tell us the answer must be separatism. We must set our own course and defend it against those who would deny us -- just as the American colonists did in 1776 in the face of British oppression...

If there were any reason to believe that a successor to Camp would have fundamentally different views, there would be grounds for hope of a reconciliation, but there is no sign of that. Camp seems to represent majority white opinion in the North, so it is not possible for us to assume that Washington will become more reasonable in a later administration.

The black militia would do everything in its power to "halt the aggressors," the statement continued. Admitting that "the militia might not have the strength to defeat the enemy decisively," it yet warned that "by the time Camp's troops have met our resistance, they will know they can have no easy victory, and the world will know that this is a genuine war of national liberation against outside aggression. Winning freedom and independence may take us as long as it took the Vietnamese, but let no one doubt that, after 400 years of the alternatives, we have the determination to stay the course."

The statement then appealed to the United Nations and "all friendly nations" for political and material support. Finally, Dillon spoke directly to white southerners:

I have never wavered from my hope that our new black majority can win the acceptance and ultimately the friendship of whites who remain in the South. Yet I feel that I must at this critical juncture issue a warning. Some of you may hope that Camp's forces will defeat us. I cannot tell you what you must in your hearts hope or believe. But if you feel moved to take up arms to help him, I ask that you remember that the situation in the South today is totally different from the past. You do not face a cowering minority. We are here to stay; we are united; and we will never again let ourselves be pushed around. We will not hesitate to deal ruthlessly with anyone who uses force to thwart the legitimate will of our new majority. Please keep this in mind as you decide whether or not to join the extremist fringe which we know is waiting to leap into action to support Camp the moment he moves.

Preparation of this statement was not the only thing agreed upon at the October "Farm" conference. The participants also agreed that, as soon as possible after the expected attack, the legislatures of the three states which already had black legislative majorities would convene for the purpose of passing a resolution in favor of independence for the South. The other two states could be expected to elect black majorities in November and vote their approval at the first sessions of their new legislatures. Dillon felt such a resolution would be legal, but had private doubts as to how binding it would be. As he remarked to a colleague, "Such a resolution will not provide adequate legal basis for this momentous a change. Ultimately there will probably need to be an amendment to the U.S. Constitution and a formal treaty between the governments of North and South." But Dillon was confident that once there emerged a de facto separate South, legal arrangements codifying that reality would in time follow. As Dillon later said in response to a reporter's question after the resolution was approved by the state legislatures, "I am certain that our declaration of independence from a nation which refuses to treat us as equals symbolizes an historic demographic and political shift which is irreversible." (Passage of the resolution was facilitated, as it turned out, by the fact that most white legislators, knowing that an independence motion would be offered, walked out.)

On the evening of November 9 -- just hours before his troops went into action -- President Camp had asked for media time to address the nation. He opened by declaring, "Clearly the time has come to punish the rebels and traitors who are intent upon destroying the unity of this nation." Then he revealed that earlier in the day he had issued orders to U.S. Army Commanders "to prepare to occupy critical locations in the South, disband the rebellious state governments and arrest rebel politicians who are plainly intent on subverting the U.S. Constitution." The troops would move within a few hours, he said. Those already stationed at southern bases would operate from those bases, while four divisions in bordering states were at that moment preparing to cross the borders of the rebellious states; other units would be airlifted south during the next few days.

At that time, about 11 percent of the Army was black, a reduction from 18 percent in 2017 when the regular Army was first sent into the ghettoes. Camp decreed that any black soldier who did not wish to participate in operations in the South could request discharge immediately, retaining whatever veteran's rights and benefits he had accumulated up to that time. But any who remained in the Army would be expected to perform as ordered or be subject to court-martial.

The 14th Infantry Division, stationed in eastern Texas, was assigned the task of occupying Baton Rouge, the capital of Louisiana. The division had already moved up to the Texas-Louisiana border by dusk on November 9. Just after midnight, the division's commanding general sent his troops across the border into Louisiana, where they planned to move along Interstate 10 to Baton Rouge. Apparently the general still couldn't quite believe that he was about to enter a real shooting war, so the entire division consisted of a miles-long convoy of armored personnel carriers, trucks, tanks, buses and jeeps. A few miles inside Louisiana, black militia forces blew up a bridge just as the division approached. The bridge crossed a bayou in a swampy area where it was virtually impossible for the convoy's vehicles to operate.

The black militia leaders had, not surprisingly, been aware of the division's movement to the border during the preceding hours, and in the swamps had positioned over 4,000 men and women with an arsenal of small arms including everything from hunting rifles to bazookas and machine guns bought in the international arms market. Just as the bridge blew up, the black militia opened fire on the convoy. Some of the militia were firing from small rowboats in the swamp, others from behind trees or small islands of mud and sand. The soldiers were able to aim effective fire at those militia members who fell within their searchlights, but most of the militia were well-camouflaged and the northern troops were at their mercy. Northern infantrymen dismounted from their vehicles and entered the swamp, but movement was difficult and they made easy targets. It can be said that the northern counter-attack never really got off the ground before the commanding general called for a retreat, only 20 minutes after the battle began. The general used loudspeakers to tell the black militia that if they would cease firing, the convoy would retreat back across the Texas border. He had been stunned at the unexpected loss of life, and felt certain that it was not the intention of the U.S. leadership (and certainly not his intention) to push ahead in the face of determined resistance and with the certainty of large-scale bloodshed. He now knew that the intelligence briefing he received from the Pentagon had been woefully inadequate: it had predicted an immediate collapse of the black militia's "token resistance" the moment it faced the firepower of an organized Army division. And he could now see that if in fact putting down the rebellion justified military action, then an entirely different level of preparation and a new strategy would be called for.

Upon hearing the general's offer to retreat, militia leaders ordered an immediate cease-fire and told the convoy it could gather its dead, attend its wounded and retreat in safety. The result of this bloody confrontation was the loss of over 300 lives in the northern forces and some 200 among the black militia.

Throughout the pre-dawn hours of November 10, other Army units had been moving into position to occupy strategic objectives. On the black side, meanwhile, both rural and urban militia units had been moving to assembly points to prepare for action. Some thousands of white vigilantes, knowing that action was imminent, were grabbing their rifles and trying to contact someone who could tell them where to go in order to help the Army. These included WCLC members, KKK members, and an assortment of what were generally referred to as "rednecks." But all of these vigilantes, to the extent they were hoping to see action in defense of a white South, were to be disappointed. For before they could be usefully deployed, the "war" was over. Before any further operations could be launched, the airwaves became filled with news of the Interstate 10 incident -- along with reports on the early reaction to it in Washington. This reaction in the national capital changed the political context entirely.

When news of the battle reached Washington, there occurred what newsmen described as "sheer panic." Almost no one in Congress, it seemed, expected or wanted a real shooting war between North and South, even a Dillon-led South. Even Camp's most hawkish supporters had been thinking of nothing riskier than a somewhat expanded exercise in ghetto-type martial law. Camp immediately began hearing words of caution against stumbling into a full-scale civil war along racial lines.

In retrospect it can be seen that Camp had not kept up with rapidly evolving public opinion since 2018. Even he later admitted this. We now know that by late 2020, a large number of people in the

North were unwilling to support a costly and bloody effort to hold on to the South; some were, in fact, willing -- even eager -- to write off the South entirely. This shift could not have been predicted before 2018, and it is likely that even in mid-2019 a poll on the future of the South would have shown the great majority saying they favored using any means, including force, to prevent Southern secession. By the first half of 2020, however, with black majorities growing steadily in the South, one began to hear quite different views. A typical argument was: "We already have a nearly complete separation of the races in our large cities, so why not a de facto separation along state lines, as long as the minority rights of southern whites are protected. The situation would actually be more favorable than in the cities, because whereas economically devastated and socially unstable black cities existing as alienated islands within white-dominated states can not possibly be welded into viable communities, entire states under African-American control would have the basis, at least, for viability. If black state governments failed to build prosperity and move toward economic equality for blacks, then blacks would have no one to blame but themselves. It would be quite different from existing conditions in the black-majority northern cities, where African-American mayors have never had any real chance of controlling the political or economic environment in which the cities existed."

Such arguments began to crop up quite frequently in letters to the editor in northern papers. Whether the writers at that time went so far as to consider full independence for a black South would be hard to say, but if they did, they said it mostly in private conversation rather than in print.

In the aftermath of the Interstate 10 incident, the Congressional tide swung overwhelmingly in favor of calling off the "police action," and Camp's Capitol Hill friends descended on the White House to impress upon him the strength of anti-war sentiment in Congress and throughout the country. They explained that to the northern man-in-the-street, the radical black ascendancy had turned the South into what for all practical purposes seemed a separate entity with interests fundamentally different from those "at home." Furthermore, since there was no chance that the racial shift could be reversed, it did not seem worth fighting to hold onto the region, as victory would simply assure the perpetuation of the same racial conflicts that had been disrupting the nation all along.

At first Camp could hardly believe his ears. Here were even his most supportive Congressional backers telling him he had let himself get badly out of touch with public opinion. As he told one group of Congressmen on November 11, "Ever since grade school, I have always believed Abraham Lincoln was our greatest hero for preserving the union, and I never met anyone who disagreed. I never imagined I would hear loyal Americans say he was wrong."

This, of course, was not the point; Lincoln was right for his time and his situation, one Congressional leader answered, but in 2020 "there were more important things than maintaining an artificial unity where real unity no longer existed."

The arguments raged throughout the nation and most vigorously in the White House Oval Office throughout the 10th, 11th and 12th. Military commanders who were stalled in their tracks besieged the Pentagon with requests for guidance. But for a while there was none, and the generals could only tell their units to sit where they were and wait until Washington could sort things out.

Once over his initial shock, President Camp also acknowledged that there might be real advantages in solving America's racial problems through geographic partition. And he admitted that in recent months, such an idea had occurred to him as he could now see it had occurred to many others -- but to him it had occurred at that time only as an evil notion to be firmly rejected.

Yet, as he told another Congressional group, even if one admitted there were advantages to some form of separation, he still couldn't see why there would have to be total independence for a black nation, rather than simply separate status within a federal union -- i.e. something like the status of Quebec in Canada or of the constituent republics in what was left of the Soviet Union. In this he was strongly supported by his white southern friends. His northern friends contended, however, that while they too would like to see such an outcome, the choice would have to be made by the South, which now meant the black South. In short, preserving the union was not worth a war, and barring a military solution, the North had no way to impose its will on the South. As even the southern whites admitted, there was no way to halt the shift to overwhelming black majorities and black-majority governments which would inevitably put black interests first. In the end, Camp, his northern congressional friends and their southern colleagues all agreed that the wisest thing for Washington to do would be to try to create the conditions which would help the South decide there were greater benefits in unity than in separation. The outcome would be uncertain, but it seemed a better choice than immediate civil war.

After three days of White House discussions during which Camp, his cabinet and the top Congressional leadership got almost no sleep, the participants finally hammered out a statement explaining the government's position.

Speaking to a huge TV audience despite the late hour (11:00 p.m. Eastern time on November 12), the President informed the nation that he had ordered an end to military operations because it had become plain that the only outcome of further use of arms would be needless bloodshed and a hardening of positions. The future of the South, he said, must depend on the will of the people in the region "who are now and will surely remain primarily black." He hoped the South would "reconsider the rather extreme statement read two days ago by Mr. Dillon and rescind the unfortunate resolutions favoring independence which were passed so hastily by three southern legislatures. All of us -- and particularly our fellow American citizens of all races in the South -- will benefit if the black-majority states remain as loyal, free, equal and prosperous states of the union." In any case, he went on, whatever political arrangements the South decided upon, "It would be madness for the region to cut off economic and cultural ties with the North." Then, in somber tones, he stated there was but one qualification to all that he had said: "The North cannot stand idly by if whites who remain in the South are denied equal rights; this government will use any and all means necessary to assure that this does not happen."

Reaction Among Southern Whites

The use of force by the white resistance in the South was, as we have seen, sidetracked by the quick collapse of Camp's attempt at a military solution -- a collapse due to two factors: first, no one really wanted a civil war; second, public opinion in the North and Camp himself, once confronted with a de facto black South, shifted in favor of accepting the new reality as the least bad of several unpalatable possibilities.

Nevertheless, the white population in the South obviously could not easily accept the new secession. It will be recalled that many white southern moderates had played down their opposition to Dillon when he first arrived in the South. True, they strongly disapproved of his call for an influx of northern ghettoites, which they felt could only make their lives less secure; they felt it would certainly lead to increased crime, as well as increased taxation to deal with all the social needs of people with few resources and skills; and, of course, there was the traumatic political prospect of becoming a minority. But these whites knew the black population was going to increase anyway, and among them were many who sympathized with Dillon's call for a black moral and social renaissance. They knew things could not go on as before, and saw a black community led by a purposeful leader as not necessarily more harmful to their long-term interests than one that sank further into alienation, frustration and chaos because of a lack of purpose or hope. These whites wanted to reach a *modus vivendi* that, while recognizing black majorities as inevitable, would allow daily life for themselves to continue with only minor change.

But even among white moderates, needless to say, there were few, if any, who supported Dillon's move toward complete separation. When this occurred, some who had remained on the sidelines joined the active white resistance, while others, who perhaps had already been contemplating leaving the South, were catalyzed by secession to do so. A third group, quite large, also abominated the notion of a separate black-ruled South, yet had no inclination to use violence to stop it; nor was departure a solution, as they could not bear to leave their homes, property and traditions. They were mired in indecision. Not knowing which way to move, they sullenly remained in place. They would wait it out, letting unfolding events decide their fate for them. By 2023, many of these people were still in the South, and were gradually learning to live with the new reality -- no matter how unpleasant they found it.

In the days following passage of the independence resolution by the newly elected black legislative majorities, hooded Klansmen and burning crosses popped up all across the South, and numerous assassination attempts occurred. Dillon was shot at twice, but from a distance, and the only result was a shoulder injury to one of his body-guards. However a total of 14 lesser black leaders -- all of whom had been outspokenly pro-Dillon -- were assassinaetd. Angry black militia members responded in kind, resulting in eight deaths and several injuries among acknowledged Klansmen and their mediagenic front-men. One of those assassinated was a South Carolina Congressman who, despite his soothing TV voice and well-tailored business suits, was widely known to have close contacts with the Klan.

At the same time, among the less-violent white resistance, there were attempts at covert action, mainly by offering bribes to black leaders to turn against Dillon. Ever since 2017, there had been a white-funded disinformation campaign using bribery to get blacks to spread rumors about financial and sexual misconduct by Dillon. But the chief result was that the black participants, in exchange for pocket change, got themselves branded as Uncle Toms and lost credibility with the African-American community. This continued to be true now, despite the willingness of angry whites to make much greater funds available for such schemes.

Although few blacks would cooperate with white efforts to oppose Dillon, even for big money, it cannot be said that there was no black opposition. Serious doubts about the wisdom of Dillon's confrontational politics were not uncommon in private conversation and could occasionally be discerned between the lines in public discourse. But Dillon had drawn a political line in the sand, and almost all African-Americans in the South stood on his side of it; few others, whatever their private doubts, thought it wise to stand publicly on the other side.

How Northern Conditions Affected the South

In looking back on the events of 2020, it seems ironic that while it was the South that was fundamentally transformed, it was the problems in the North that precipitated the process. Because of the gradual improvement in race relations in the South in the preceding decades, it is possible that a viable, genuinely power-sharing two-race society could have developed there. Not all white southerners had abandoned racist views, to be sure, but the changes since the 1960's had been enormous. Most members of both races had come to feel that they had no choice but to get along, because that was the only hope for a decent future for themselves and their children in the South. It is possible that there might even have occurred a peaceful and cooperative transition to the black majorities which would eventually have come about in any case if the black birth rate had continued higher than the white. But the failure to solve the problems of the urban ghettoes outside of the South made such an opportunity for evolutionary change impossible. By 2016 the majority of blacks lived in urban ghettoes, and the system had no means either to integrate them into the broader society or to transform the ghettoes into decent and viable communities. Ultimately blacks had to escape the impossible conditions of the ghettoes, and there was no place to escape to other than the South, where they could believe they had at least some roots in the land.

CHAPTER FIVE

THE HISPANIC SOUTHWEST, 2016-2020

In his 2016 campaign, Andrew Camp had called not only for putting down the black rebellion in the ghettoes, but also for controlling immigration from abroad and expelling all illegal immigrants from U.S. territory. And upon his inauguration in January 2017, he set to work on the second task as well as the first. He immediately instructed the Immigration and Naturalization Service (INS) to enforce existing immigration laws to the letter, and alerted the Pentagon to be prepared to help. Then, with support from his backers in Congress, he pushed through laws to put a virtual end even to legal immigration, with only rare exceptions for special circumstances. The immigration halt was, of course, aimed primarily at Hispanics.

By this time, the rapid growth of the Hispanic population was on the verge of leading to Hispanic majorities in both Texas and California, and it was plain that a continuation of existing trends would lead to very large majorities within a generation. Furthermore, the speed of the ethnic shift was steadily increasing as ever greater numbers fled north from the revolutions that began in Central America and then spread to Mexico and parts of South America. The fact that the white-Anglo population had a low birth rate and was aging rapidly (the average age of Anglos in California was more than 15 years above that of Hispanics by 2010) also contributed to the speed of the demographic shift.

In both states, the Hispanic population was concentrated primarily in the southern halves, with Anglos in the north determined to keep their regions English-speaking. In California, in particular, there had been a number of incidents of racism and violence growing out of attempts by Hispanics to settle farther north, with the result that the great majority of Hispanics had decided to remain in the south where the culture and language had become predominantly, and in some areas almost exclusively, Hispanic. In southern California, from about 2010 on, some Anglos and Asians, and even some blacks, had come to feel uncomfortable in what seemed an increasingly foreign society, and made the difficult decision to leave. But the outflow had not yet developed into the nearly unanimous white flight that had occurred from the northern inner cities, and the great majority of Anglos had no desire to leave the climatically delightful region where they continued to control most of the economy and where many enjoyed comfortable homes with low-cost illegal immigrant servants. Yet by 2016, some observers were already predicting that as Hispanic political and cultural dominance grew, the impetus among Anglos to seek more kindred surroundings would likewise grow.

As for the other border states, New Mexico of course had long had an Hispanic majority; that left Arizona, which in 2016 was still predominantly Anglo. Yet it was apparent that the high Hispanic birth rate combined with the large illegal immigration following the Latin American revolutions would lead to an Hispanic majority even in Arizona before mid-century.

Following Camp's orders, the INS, backed by Army troops, did make an attempt to control the U.S.-Mexican border and to round up and expel illegal aliens. But the attempt was short-lived and half-hearted. The INS received very little cooperation from the Hispanic community, while the military found almost no illegals at all -- even in the rare instances when the troops reached their destinations. More often than not, Army units were stopped by barricades thrown up by Hispanic communities and never reached their destinations. The troops almost never tried to break through the barricades by force because their commanders knew the whole effort was perfunctory and that few, if any, illegals would be found; furthermore, even if those few were expelled at the border, they would be helped back into the U.S. within hours by the groups which specialized in smuggling such people.

Camp and his supporters were frustrated and angered by the failure of the effort, but it was not long before their attention was fully absorbed by the black ghettoes, where violent rebellion was an on-going daily crisis. With the Administration's energies diverted, the immigration effort was allowed to expire virtually unnoticed within nine months, although the President never formally admitted it was dead.

Although poverty and violent crime were not strangers to the Hispanic barrios and farms of the Southwest, social and political conditions were not identical to those in the black ghettoes. Whereas the ghettoes had no economic or social basis for the formation of viable communities, the Hispanic regions exhibited many of the elements of real communities -- albeit often with an appearance more akin to the Third World than to the industrialized countries of Europe, Asia and most of North America. By 2016, millions of people lived in rural farm-hand shacks or depressed urban neighborhoods resembling the slums of Mexico City or Rio de Janiero more than the middle class neighborhoods of America. But the residents even of such depressed areas as these could feel that they were a part of the broader Hispanic society which surrounded them. They could travel through both urban and rural areas with the knowledge that they were in a culture that in large part accepted them and spoke their language. This was quite unlike the situation of a northern African-American ghettoite who long had felt that if he dared to wander into a white neighborhood at all, he was being watched by suspicious eyes which saw in him the evil virus of ghetto violence and social breakdown.

So the Hispanic community appeared to have a certain long-term potential for survival within the existing federal structure of the United States; and had the population and territory of Hispanic predominance been stabilized, it might eventually have done so. The problem was the rapid growth of the population. By this time, the nation's Hispanics numbered 56 million, with 38 million in the Southwest.

The southwestern Hispanic community gave the appearance of being an essentially Mexican one. That is, it consisted of people who were either of Mexican extraction or, if from other Latin American countries, were in the process of being absorbed into the region's predominantly Mexican "melting pot." The Central Americans were absorbed almost immediately, while those from other parts of Latin America took somewhat longer. The approximately 18 million Hispanics outside of the Southwest tier of states were mostly in Florida (primarily Cubans), in the large northern cities (notably New York and Chicago), or in the southern counties of Colorado just north of the New Mexican border. In all, Hispanics constituted approximately 8 percent of the total U.S. population outside of the southwestern states.

The Hispanic numbers in the southwestern states were far from being fully reflected in the November 2016 election results, because so many were ineligible to vote and the percentage even of qualified voters who actually went to the polls continued to be low. By two years later, however, the situation had begun to change. From 2016 to 2018, Manuel Rivera and other Hispanic leaders had watched carefully as the African-American revolution and King Dillon's southern migration developed. They began to push harder than ever for Hispanics to go to the polls, arguing that their numbers could prove just as decisive in the Southwest as black numbers were proving to be in the South. This new effort to get Hispanics to vote was relatively successful, and in 2018, Hispanics won over 60 percent of the Congressional seats up for election in the Hispanic-majority region of the Southwest, plus a similar percentage of state and local offices. (This was in spite of the fact that perhaps one-third of the Hispanic community did not have citizenship and hence could not vote.) Rivera himself was elected to the U.S. House of Representatives, after having been out of office since he resigned from the California Senate to run for the U.S. Senate in 2016. The election results gave great encouragement to the Hispanic-nationalist element among Hispanic leaders, including Rivera, who was the most widely recognized and often quoted among them.

In his post-2018 speeches, Rivera argued strongly and persis-tently that the time had arrived for putting Spanish on an equal footing with English in the southwestern states and that eventually it should be given equal official status on the national level. In addition, in speech after speech he contended that the gap in wealth between Hispanics and Anglos was unacceptable. He said it was the direct result of the fact that Anglos still owned most of the sources of wealth -- that is, the land and property -- of the Southwest. Therefore Hispanics should acquire wealth-producing property at every oppor-tunity, and state legislatures should consider tax policies similar to those advocated by King Dillon to fund the programs that would attack the educational and social causes of inequality. He always appealed directly to his listeners' sense of historical grievance, not letting them forget that, as he saw it, their ancestors had arrived in the region first and present inequalities were "the direct result of past Anglo aggression and robbery."

Anglos, both in the Southwest and elsewhere, vehemently denounced Rivera's "demagoguery." Many observed that the prime cause of existing poverty was the influx of immigrants who brought their developing world standards into this country and kept wages and standards low. In fact, by this time, minimum wage laws were simply ignored in much of the Southwest, whether in agricultural areas or in cities, as desperate refugees were eager to work for any wage at all. Send the illegal immigrants back to their home countries, Anglos said, and over time the Anglo population could work with American Hispanics to raise the living standards of the latter to equal levels. But few people actually believed the immigrants would ever depart, and as Anglos in the Southwest faced ever more clearly the prospect of becoming a minority amidst a predominantly non-English-speaking population, their concerns about the future grew.

In an interview in mid-2019, a year and a half before the North-South split, Rivera gave the author his assessment of where he thought the U.S. was going at that time: "I think the authority of the national government has broken down, probably terminally. There is anarchy in the northern cities, and there seems to be no solution. A black-white war seems more likely than not. It would be nice if it could be avoided, but there is nothing we here in the Southwest can do about it. What happens in the East doesn't affect us directly, but the North-South conflict means Washington isn't even going to notice the needs of Hispanics out here, much less do anything about them. Clearly, we are going to have to solve our own problems. Now, if we can't expect any help from Washington, neither will we stand for any interference if Washington doesn't like some of the things we do -- language laws, tax laws, the way we handle the immigration question, that sort of thing."

2020: *Conflict in the Hispanic Community*

All during 2020, Hispanic leaders continued to watch the polarization between Andrew Camp's North and King Dillon's South. When the split actually occurred in November, Rivera spent little time lamenting the United States' loss of the South. In fact, upon considering the implications of events back east, he concluded that the split created a new opportunity for the Southwest -- one he had not previously thought existed.

In discussing this "new opportunity" with his followers, Rivera reminded them, as always, that Anglos had never really accepted Hispanics as equal partners in America and, he added, they never would. Hispanics should no longer have to suffer the indignities of being poor and second-class citizens in their own country, and the only way to avoid this would be for the Hispanic Southwest to do as the South had done: to make a complete break with the English-speaking states of the North and establish their own political entity, whatever form it might take. True, Hispanics already had -- or were well on their way to having -- their own separate cultural and linguistic region, but politically and economically, they were still virtually powerless. Most important, Rivera went on, the Camp Administration's failure to make the sacrifices needed to hold on to the South indicated it probably also lacked the will to fight to preserve an Hispanic Southwest determined to set its own separate course. Finally, he admitted that he had always had a vision of a new Hispanic nation in the Southwest, free at last from the "foreign" domination that began long ago with Anglo aggression in the Mexican War. He claimed that many other Hispanics also longed for this but, like him, had never in the past been able to let themselves believe it might be possible.

When such thoughts began to find their way into Rivera's public speeches, they generated a certain response in the barrios. Enthusiastic political graffiti and banners appeared, while demonstrations and rallies in favor of "reclaiming our land," "Hispanic power," and even "independence for Aztlan" became the meat of daily headlines. ("Aztlan" was a pre-Columbian name for northern Mexico, and had been adopted in the late 20th Century by certain Latino extremists for their dreamed-of Hispanic homeland.) Many observers no doubt took these demonstrations as a vigorous sign of support for Rivera's now openly-expressed dream. But the reality was that the great majority of Hispanics had no desire to follow as far as Rivera was now ready to lead.

It was not that they opposed Rivera personally; polls continued to show that he enjoyed a "favorable" rating among a majority of Hispanics. But the size of the majority had dropped noticeably since the days when he had been talking merely of making Spanish official or pushing for economic opportunity and "Hispanic power" in the Southwest -- none of which required a complete split with the rest of the nation. In fact, the prospect of such a split had scarcely entered the consciousness of the ordinary Hispanic by the time Rivera began advocating it.

We now know that the demonstrations and banners in support of Rivera's new line were the work of a well-organized radical nationalist minority which was able to enlist some thousands of students and other young people to create enough of a clamor to attract the attention of the TV cameras. As for the great majority of Hispanics, they just wanted to get on with their lives -- no matter how happy they had been and still were to see Rivera or anyone else in a leadership role pressuring the Anglo power structure to open more doors for Hispanic equality and respect.

One person who was shocked by Rivera's new line was Carlos Ortiz, the governor of New Mexico, who had been a close associate of the Californian until a year before, when he had come to feel that Rivera was beginning to say things that would make cooperation more difficult both with Washington and with Anglos residing in the Southwest. Ortiz had then drifted away from Rivera, although up to the time of Rivera's public shift to complete separatism following the secession of the South, there had been no public break between them.

In Ortiz' view, although Hispanics were indeed on the verge of becoming the dominant population group in the Southwest, the fact remained that the southwestern states were an arbitrarily and artificially defined territory. There was no way such a territory could go it alone, he said. As he observed in one speech, "Rivera's glib talk of going our own separate way not only is extreme and unfair historically and politically, but totally ignores such hard economic realities as the skills, capital, markets and resources needed for separate nationhood." Then he asked rhetorically, "What would happen, for instance, if the North, in anger at a secessionist Hispanic region, refused to honor the Colorado River Pact and used more than its designated share of water?" Answering his own question, he said: "The Southwest would simply dry up, that's what." He continued, "The present and future prosperity of the Hispanic region depends on its economy being fully integrated with the markets and resources of the North, and that requires political integration and cooperation. To cut these ties would bring disaster to the Southwest and permanent impoverishment to our people."

"In reality," Ortiz concluded, "reversion to Mexico might well become the fate of an Hispanic Southwest cut off from the U.S. Would the people of the region willingly accept that? After all, in just the last decade, millions of Mexicans have fled to the U.S. Southwest for the specific purpose of fleeing the chaos of Mexico's revolution."

Thus, as the end of 2020 approached, the debate went on in the Southwest between those who, like Ortiz, wanted the Southwest to become a Quebec-type predominantly Spanish-speaking region within the United States and those who, like Rivera and his circle, were now arguing that complete separation was the only way to end second-class status for Hispanics, Hispanic culture and the Spanish language.

The debate in the Southwest was not the only one occurring at this time in regard to the Hispanic region. The one going on in Washington was equally intense, though at first less public.

It will be recalled that up to November, Andrew Camp had been prepared to go to war to prevent the black South from breaking away. What halted the attempt was a swing in public and Congressional opinion which convinced Camp not only that a war to prevent a split was a higher price than Americans were willing to pay, but that the loss of the South could even have a positive side as it would remove from white America the problem of dealing with an unassimilable black minority. By the end of December 2020, the advantages of giving up the black South had come to seem even more apparent to Camp, who now for the first time in years could turn his full attention to the many other problems long submerged by the guerrilla warfare in the cities.

Among these problems was how to deal with the Hispanic Southwest, with its rapidly-growing non-English-speaking population. Although English was still spoken by more people than Spanish in the region, it was clear that the growth of the Spanish-speaking element would soon change this. The more Camp pondered the Hispanic question, the more he became convinced that it, like that of blacks, could not be solved satisfactorily within the framework of existing American politics.

As the cabinet and Congressional leaders discussed the issue during the early weeks of the new year, Camp and those who agreed with him made frequent mention of the advantages the racially and culturally more homogeneous societies like those of East Asia and Europe seemed to be enjoying over the U.S. The fortunate in those countries looked upon the less fortunate as being essentially like themselves and saw efforts to help them as "helping their own kind;" those in a position to help could imagine that they, given a slight change in the wheel of fortune, might themselves need help -- or if not them, their children or grandchildren. The fortunate white-Anglo in America, on the contrary, tended to see help to the minorities as, at best, conscience money or an attempt to buy good behavior or, at worst, money thrown down a rathole. It was very hard for an affluent white suburbanite to identify with a black ghettoite or a Mexican lettuce picker in the way a rich Swede or Japanese could identify with a poor Swede or Japanese. Consequently, while the more homogeneous countries were able to devote their energies to an across-the-board raising of educational, economic and cultural standards, the U.S.'s political energies tended to be dissipated in angry futility and in countering the poverty and lawlessness that resulted from racial and ethnic prejudice and inequality. Furthermore, the availability of cheap "developing world" labor pouring into the U.S. reduced the incentives to modernization and helped keep overall economic and educational standards from catching up to the advanced countries of Europe and Asia.

As Camp and his people pursued these lines of thought, the fact that the once-sacred unity of the United States had already been sacrificed with the loss of the South made it easier to contemplate the idea of the nation being further reduced in territory by the loss of another unassimilable region. As Camp remarked at one cabinet meeting, "Perhaps the time has come to solve the nation's racial and ethnic divisions once and for all, and for what is left of the United States to start again with a new and more cohesive basis for national unity."

Camp acknowledged that the break between the Anglo and Hispanic regions which he was now leaning toward would be exceedingly wrenching. Many Anglos, both in the North and in the Southwest, would bitterly, probably violently, oppose it. But the alternative could only be worse, he argued. The continued existence of a rapidly-growing minority which was in part living at Developing World standards and which spoke a different language could only lead to increased friction and ultimately to some sort of Anglo-Hispanic split on terms less favorable geographically to the Anglo population. "If a split is to occur," the President is quoted as having said, "let it happen now."

In late January, there appeared on the *New York Times* Op-ed page a piece which argued that the breakup of the United States along racial and ethnic lines had become historically inevitable. The author was one Arden Crump, of whom no one appears to have heard before or since -- but a low-ranking member of the National Security Council is said to have revealed unofficially that he was none other than President Camp. "Crump" admitted that recently there had been an enormous change in his own thinking on the question of racial and ethnic divisions:

> A year ago, this writer would have branded anyone advocating a breakup of the United States a traitor, but now I see it differently. I admit that my personal change of view would strike some people as shockingly swift, but given the new realities that had emerged in recent years, I think the clean break with the black South is better for all concerned; and I don't see how some kind of separatism between English-speaking and Spanish-speaking regions can be avoided over the long term...
>
> Americans have long observed the ethnic, religious and racial divisions in other countries with a certain smugness. We could easily understand how such divisions could shatter the cohesion of the Soviet Union, South Africa, Yugoslavia, India or Lebanon. But the U.S. melting pot was seen as immune to such disruptions. 'After all, we're all immigrants,' we Americans like to tell ourselves, and we were brought up to believe that once the first-generation immigrants in our family trees reached American shores,

every future generation would be fully American in its loyalties; it didn't matter whether your ancestors were English, German, Greek, Russian, Catholic, Jewish or, more recently, Asian. But two groups have always been in a different situation. The majority of blacks had never been assimilated and integrated despite the fact that their forebears had been on American shores far longer than those of most whites, while Hispanics were fully 'melted' only if they looked at least partly European and spoke English. In recent decades, with the flood of non-English speakers from Latin America, the Hispanic community, instead of moving toward eventual assimilation, has been moving steadily farther away from it.

The recently-surfaced desire first of blacks and now of Hispanics for self-rule should not surprise anyone who has studied world history. Throughout history, minority ethnic, racial and linguistic loyalties have been shown to be stronger than loyalties to a multi-ethnic nation-state wherever the minority has seen the values, traditions and daily life experience of the majority group as significantly different from its own. The Soviet Union is a conspicuous example of this in modern times. Despite decades of post-Revolution propaganda about the 'fraternal peoples' of the Soviet Union, once the threat of punishment was removed from the expression of ethnic identity -- as Mikhail Gorbachev realized it had to be if ever the Soviet Union were to move beyond the primitive authoritarianism of the past -- the underlying ethnic divisions immediately came to the surface. Suddenly the rest of the world became aware that millions of Soviet citizens saw themselves as Armenians, Estonians or Uzbekis first, and Soviet citizens second.

The situation in the U.S. is comparable. The potential for a separate black or Hispanic identity and loyalty has always been there. Polls have long shown that many blacks and Hispanics identified with and felt loyalty toward their own ethnic community first, and the nation as a whole, second. And this is hardly surprising, given the experience of their daily lives. As for ghetto blacks, in recent decades they had almost no contact with whites, and on the rare occasions when they did, it was likely to involve confrontation and conflict. The society they knew first-hand was entirely black and far removed from the traditions and daily realities of the majority culture. As for Hispanic separateness, it is mostly cultural and linguistic, but these can be barriers no easier to remove than the racial ones between black and white.

In reality, it must be recognized that the U.S. racial and ethnic problem had by last November become more severe even than the Soviet in one critical respect, namely that the educational, social and eocnomic gap between the main ethnic groups in the U.S. was greater than in the U.S.S.R., which meant that the tendency toward feelings of superiority by some and alienated inferiority by others was likewise greater.

Despite the long-standing existence of latent nationalisms among American blacks and Hispanics, the implications for national unity have until recently been hidden. In the past, the minorities were sufficiently few in number that neither they nor white-Anglos could have taken seriously a minority attempt to pressure the majority into granting them a separate political territory. Any such attempt would have been quickly suppressed, and all sides knew it. But in the last few decades, the situation has changed fundamentally -- although right up to last November, many of us had failed to recognize it. With the low white birth rate, the relatively high minority birth rate and the massive immigration, the minorities had become such a large proportion of the total population that the white-Anglo majority could no longer automatically quash incipient separatist tendencies... The system, in fact, could no longer survive without the full participation and assimilation of the minorities -- yet there was no way to gain this.

We may safely take these views as representative of President Camp, whether or not the words were actually written by him. In any case, we know from later statements by participants in White House discussions during this period that similar arguments were vigorously put forth by Camp and those who sided with him. And we also know that there was a vigorous negative reaction to them from some top Washington insiders -- using words so strong, in fact, that they led to fisticuffs at one White House meeting attended by the cabinet and congressmen from the southwestern states.

With such bitter divisions existing among the political leaders in Washington, it didn't take long for the debate to go public. But in an effort to avoid excessive personal exposure on such a sensitive issue, Camp decided to stay in the background and let his secretary of commerce, Sylvia Phillips, become the chief public spokesperson for the President's views. Her remarks on the news and in interview programs generated a nationwide uproar which rather quickly answered -- with a resounding "no" -- the question of whether the Southwest would, as she and Camp favored, be pushed down the independent path taken by the black South.

The most vocal opposition understandably came from Anglo residents of the southwestern states. Northern Californians, particularly, said they would never accept being cut off from the U.S. and would take up arms to prevent it. And Anglos in southern California as well as the other concerned states indicated solidarity with them. In the northern states, Phillips received a fair amount of support for her (and Camp's) view that a split now would be easier to swallow than a less advantageous (i.e. to Anglos) split later or an attempt to deal indefinitely with a growing and increasingly unassimilable minority. Yet it was plain that this support constituted less than a majority, even in the North. Although the Camp/Phillips school, having sacrificed the South, was now willing to "settle the racial and ethnic dilemma once and for all," many other Americans had been moved quite differently by the loss of the South, and now raised their hackles at the thought of any further carving-up of the United States.

The reaction of Anglos, both in the Southwest and elsewhere, could not entirely have been a surprise to Camp, since their point of view had been so vigorously reflected in the earlier discussions held at the White House. But he was no doubt surprised by the reaction among Hispanics. One week after Secretary Phillips' first "trial balloon" went up on the TV news, a bloody melee occurred at a Los Angeles rally held by Manuel Rivera, at which about 500 anti-Rivera Hispanics attacked him and some 200 of his supporters -- leaving Rivera among four dead. The assault appears to have been spontaneous, and no one has yet been punished for it. Governor Ortiz expressed condolences for his former colleague, though he still pointedly accused him of having been led astray by "unrealistic dreams of an Hispanic nation free of the past and, apparently, free of the realities of present and future."

The Los Angeles incident served as a catalyst to bring Hispanic feelings and loyalties into the open, and although there was no lack of grief for Rivera personally, it was clear that his recent ideas had not caught on. Parades of Hispanic-American military veterans in now ill-fitting uniforms, and American flags proudly protruding from front porches, were among the visible patriotic symbols much in evidence on barrio streets, as the anti-separatists tried to send the message to Camp and the rest of the nation that most Hispanics strongly opposed a split.

In late February, Governor Ortiz led a delegation of Hispanic leaders to Washington, and over the course of 13 days worked out with the Camp Administration and the leaders of Congress a proposal for the future of the Southwest.

Although President Camp now had no choice but to back off from his notion that the Hispanic question could be solved by removing the Hispanic-majority states from the nation, once he did so, he found that he had plenty of support on certain other issues. The Administration, Congress and, polls indicated, a clear majority of the people now insisted that immigration be controlled, that English retain its status as the official language of their land, and that welfare and all other policies which encouraged or merely failed to discourage "irresponsible breeding" be changed; "irresponsible breeding" was, of course, a code word for the high birth rate among those too poor to raise their children without public assistance -- and there is little doubt that those who used the term were thinking primarily of the minorities. The question was, how could these requirements be met while preserving the union of the Anglo North and an Hispanic-dominated Southwest. These were the issues congressional and Administration leaders brought to the talks with Governor Ortiz and his team, who also had their minimum demands.

The Hispanic contingent maintained that the Spanish language had become as common as English in most of the Southwest and its use could not be suppressed. Therefore, it had to be given a status at least equal to English in all official dealings in their region, from legislative debates to road signs to classroom use. Furthermore if, as seemed certain, the demographic evolution of the southwestern states were to lead in the future to Spanish becoming the primary language in the region, then that reality must also be accepted. There must be no outside interference to hinder the evolution of Spanish into a position comparable to that of French in Quebec -- if that turned out to be the result of demographic change. In essence, Ortiz was implying, the predominant language of the Southwest was going to become Spanish and the North was going to have to learn to live with it. In addition to the language issue, Ortiz pointed out that "Hispanic power" would be an inevitable by-product of growing Hispanic numbers, and it had to be understood that this power would be used to promote Hispanic culture and to move toward economic equality for Hispanics. Finally, there must be no demographic or immigration policy which in any way implied an Anglo effort to limit the growth of the Hispanic population.

After the negotiators had laid out what their respective sides considered essential, it was apparent that it would be impossible to satisfy both sides within the existing terms of the federal union, and that new arrangements would be necessary. The negotiators then proceeded to work out their proposal for a new status for the southwestern border states -- a proposal which was presented to Congress and the American people in April 2021 and became a constitutional reality in November 2022, following passage of a constitutional amendment by the requisite number of states.

The Hispanic Autonomous Region

The primary distinguishing characteristics of the four-state Hispanic Autonomous Region (HAR) relate to language and demographic change. (The states concerned are Texas, New Mexico, Arizona and California; a plebiscite will be held in 2027 in northern California to determine if that region will break away from southern California to form a new state outside of the HAR. Recently some Anglos in parts of northern Arizona and northern Texas have been demanding a similar plebiscite for their areas.) The status of the two major languages in the HAR will be determined by the individual states through the democratic process, with no outside intervention; precisely what the linguistic arrangements ultimately turn out to be, only time will tell. It is possible that the two languages will exist side by side indefinitely on a basis of equality, but some observers feel that over the next few decades there may be a substantial Anglo exodus from the region, which could lead to Spanish becoming overwhelmingly predominant.

Equally delicate is the question of population control. In order to remove the former concern among northern Anglos that the demographic makeup of the nation was changing at a pace too rapid for them to absorb, there are now barriers to immigration between the HAR and the rest of the nation. All persons legally in either region have U.S. citizenship, but they are in addition required to have permanent residency in one or the other of the two regions. All citizens are required to carry non-forgible identification cards bearing their fingerprints -- this despite substantial protest from the ACLU and other groups -- and they are not permitted to reside or work in the other region without official permission. These arrangements are not dissimilar to those that emerged early in this century for citizens of the republics of the U.S.S.R., the autonomous regions of China, and the tribal territories of several multi-ethnic states of Africa. To enforce the new immigration arrangements, sturdy fences have been built along the North's border with the HAR (as well as with New Africa), and border control stations have been established on all roads between the regions.

Immigration from Latin America into the HAR is controlled by the regional administration set up by the HAR Congress to deal with this and other common questions. It appears that the HAR states now have a stricter attitude toward immigration, which is not surprising, since even Manuel Rivera had admitted to the author some years ago that once Hispanics were assured power in their region, continued Developing World immigration would be politically unnecessary and counterproductive in terms of raising economic and educational standards. At the present time, the HAR has already begun to control the southern border effectively, though there are no indications that present HAR residents who arrived illegally will be expelled.

With the exception of these language and residency arrangements, the economic, constitutional and political terms of the federal union have not changed significantly with the inauguration of the HAR. The people of the region have made clear their determination to remain part of a fully integrated national economy; to serve in the same military; to pursue no separate foreign policy (except insofar as a certain amount of independence would be required for an interim period to deal with immigration questions); to honor the same flag and other national symbols; and to study the same national history (supplemented by a regional emphasis on Hispanic studies.)

CHAPTER 6

THE PRESENT SITUATION-- 2023

===

New Africa

Since the independence of New Africa, the migration of the black and white populations has continued, with the result that today New Africa is only 28 percent white while the United States is 7 percent black. Most observers anticipate that the shift will continue, particularly of whites out of the South, but it is unlikely that the respective minorities will ever depart entirely.

A certain bitterness understandably remains among the people on both sides, and this has to date prevented any serious talk of reunification. Nevertheless, that outcome is undoubtedly still desired by a large number of people in both countries. Whether it ever occurs will have to be left to a future generation of leaders. It is unlikely to occur under King Dillon.

Despite the continued resentment over past conflicts, relations between the two countries have become more cordial in the past year. This is in part due to the concern of both governments for the minority population in the other country, but another potent factor is that the economic advantages of continued close ties are apparent to both sides, particularly New Africa.

In the first two years of New African independence, there had been almost no new investment by major corporations from the North, although virtually every significant black-owned northern business had established new branches in the South. Most of these flourished, as the need was enormous, and black consumers were eager to patronize "their own." Probably a majority of white businesses in the South as of 2020 remained, but there was a steadily growing list of closures. As part of the new climate of the past year, this has begun to change, and both sides are now talking of the value of continued and even expanded northern investment in the South. In fact, Dillon has recently gone so far as to dispatch some of his trusted advisors to the North to seek such investment.

Of considerable help to Dillon in warding off collapse in the tough months after independence was the willingness of some foreign countries to step in with aid and investment. The Arab nations in particular have been eager to invest their oil income in Western economies, including that of New Africa. They appear confident that eventually New Africa will develop economically along the hopeful lines that the South appeared to be following prior to 2013. The recently-improved North-South climate should add to this Arab confidence in the new South.

Certain African nations had followed post-2013 events in the U.S. South with great interest -- just as in the past they had seen Martin Luther King, Malcolm X, and other African-American leaders, as well as the achievements of African-Americans in general, as part of the broader black experience of which they were a part. However, with the exception of a few oil-rich nations and mineral-rich Azania, no African states have been in a position to offer anything more than moral support at the U.N. and other international forums. There has been recent talk in Africa that if present hopeful trends in New Africa continue, the latter nation may become a significant black power capable of playing a positive material and psychological role in helping the still-struggling African nations along the path to socio-economic development.

Despite the recently improved prospects, the government in New Africa is well aware that the nation will remain relatively poor for some time to come. For one thing, it is short on energy and lacks funds to buy more than a minimal share of the very expensive oil available in the international market. For another, the average economic skill level of the ex-ghettoite portion of the population at the time of independence was low for an industrialized country, and Dillon and his advisors have known from the beginning that it will take a full generation of high-quality education to bridge this gap.

In a recent visit to New Africa, this writer was encouraged by the positive spirit afoot. This has grown to no small extent out of the early successes in two areas: finding a role for previously unemployable people in the communes; and bringing relative law and order to city streets. Most ex-ghettoites are so happy to escape the drugs, street violence and guerrilla warfare of their old neighborhoods that they hardly notice that, in material terms, they have little if any more than they did in the ghettoes. Many say they are content to get by on the limited incomes presently possible because they have pride in controlling their own affairs and believe that with unity, hard work and the environmentally-sound program of economic development recently promulgated by Dillon, the nation will prosper.

The Camp Administration has taken certain steps aimed at preventing the same type of demographic tensions that existed in the past from building anew in the reduced territory of the U.S.. One step has been the total elimination of welfare support for unwed mothers and limiting to two the number of children born legitimately for whom a mother, whether or not still married, may receive welfare support. These policies are aimed equally at all races, of course, but the assumption is that they will have their greatest direct impact on the minorities. Most people of all races who might be affected by this new reality in welfare assistance have adjusted their behavior accordingly, so the change appears to have caused relatively little suffering. As for the small number of minority citizens who seem unwilling to limit the number of children they have, the Camp Administration has made it clear that they must either suffer the economic consequences of their behavior or emigrate to New Africa or the HAR.

Andrew Camp now claims he never was a racist and that he only seemed to some people to be one in the past because race was so plainly linked to the political dilemmas which were tearing the nation apart. He says he favors doing everything possible to assure equal opportunity for minority citizens remaining in the North, including offering compensatory programs in education and job training. One advantage of helping the remaining minorities rapidly achieve economic equality, he now realizes, is that the attainment of a measure of economic and social success has traditionally been the best guarantor of planned and responsible child-bearing among virtually all populations.

This is not to say, however, that all is well between the United States and the new nation of New Africa. Policy-makers in the U.S., as well as corporate leaders and the latest reports from the IMF, all point out to New Africa the inadvisability of any further pursuit of its socialist orientation, threatening an economic boycott and the refusal of credit. It is inconceivable, Andrew Camp has stressed, that the United States, having so long battled the forces of international communism, should find itself permanently confronted with a socialist state on what was once its own territory.

Whether this will have any bearing on the actions of King Dillon and of the government of New Africa remains to be seen. Undoubtedly the linkages between the two economies, plus the antagonism of the World Bank, are powerful levers. However, for obvious historical reasons the goals of "equality" and "fairness" are very strong in New Africa, and this fosters an innate preference for policies which are bound to be deemed "socialist" by pro-big-business free enterprisers. That these new policies may provide inspiration and example to low-wage workers and the poor in the

North is not likely to enhance their favor with the Camp Administration.

Dillon, however, argues that the territorial and legal changes brought about as a result of his movement and culminating in the formation of New Africa, represent nothing less than the exercise of the internationally recognized right of nationalities to self-determination. In view of the history of slavery and inequality between the African- and Anglo-Americans, territorial separation may indeed have been the only way for the former to achieve real self-determination. There is no need for continuing enmity between the peoples of New Africa and the U.S., Dillon argues; now, in fact, for the first time, the two peoples are well-positioned to enter into all the normal positive benefits of trade and cultural exchange enjoyed by countries and nationalities whose relations are grounded in equality and mutual respect. New Africa, in his view, should not be seen as a problem, but rather a solution. It should mark the beginning of a new era in which both peoples are free to pursue their economic development and the consolidation of their culture without the burden of the other. The new social forms developed by New Africa should be recognized as appropriate to a reinvigoration of the African-American cultural heritage and should expand the capacity for creative social and economic development; although these practices may not be liked, and in fact may be anathema to, the United States, they should not, Dillon feels, be seen as a threat to that country.

That post-separation views of Camp and Dillon should differ is hardly surprising. Furthermore, that such a separation could have occurred in the first place should not surprise Indian readers, given the astonishing changes that have occurred in many parts of the world since the late 20th Century.

Florida

In the years leading up to 2020, blacks had come to feel increasingly uncomfortable in Florida. Decades earlier, many of them had with difficulty learned to survive in the state's then white-dominated society and economy, only to see themselves later shoved out of traditional roles by the influx of Hispanics from Cuba and Central America. Consequently, when New Africa seceded, a good portion of the Florida black community migrated there. Their departure helped establish a solid Hispanic majority in Florida.

With the independence of New Africa, the state of Florida has been left stranded in a manner similar to Alaska, and there is now a great debate going on about the state's future. The Camp Administration has made it clear that Spanish must be replaced by English in official business, including education, if Florida is to remain in the United States. Since Spanish is the primary language in a large part of southern Florida, this will cause problems. Some Cubans and Central Americans say continued ties to the U.S. are not worth surrender on the language issue -- that not only would the shift to English be difficult to carry out, but the very notion constitutes a blatant ethnic insult. Yet the majority of Cubans probably favor continuing their present statehood status because they do not think Florida could go it alone, and there is no interest whatever in joining New Africa or becoming part of the distant HAR. Most likely, Florida will opt to retain its present status, with the Hispanic community shifting to English at the slowest pace it can get away with.

The Hispanic Autonomous Region

Although the two linguistic regions of the United States have worked together harmoniously in making the constitutional and political changes associated with the establishment of the HAR, the ultimate status of the relationship remains in some doubt. The final outcome will not be decided by the present generation, but by a future generation, and will depend on whether over time the two regions grow together or grow apart.

The essential unity of the present United States could be maintained or even strengthened if the HAR is successful in economic development, in establishing social equality and cultural pride, and in avoiding the kind of overpopulation that has been so ruinous to the economies and environments of most Latin American countries. In essence, the region must develop to the extent that Hispanics feel they can compete and cooperate on a basis of equality and mutual respect, while Anglos in the North must come to feel that there is no longer a threat of overly rapid change in the fundamental cultural and linguistic character of their region.

There has continued to be a modest exodus of Anglos (and other non-Hispanics) from the HAR. Whether it grows will depend on how Anglos are treated and whether English retains equal official status.

EPILOGUE

Could the breakup of the United States have been avoided? In theory, the answer must of course be "yes," but by 2016 conditions were such that it was probably too late to prevent it.

In order to preserve the union, the most important requirement would have been to bring the minorities fully and far more equally into the economic mainstream. Without this, the minorities could not consider American society to be truly just -- and unless they did consider it so, the society could not be stable over the long run. American democratic ideological rhetoric proclaimed that people had a right to an equal start in life and to decent rewards for leading socially responsible and economically useful lives. The reality the ghettoized minorities faced was simply too far removed from this constantly voiced but still largely, for them, theoretical ideal.

A vital step in achieving greater economic equality was to provide for all Americans the kind of quality education expected in the 21st century by citizens of the leading nations of Europe and Asia. Many, perhaps most, Americans did have this, or at least something close to it. But the minorities in the inner cities did not. To have provided it for them would have required a truly massive and unwavering commitment of the national will -- a commitment which would have been nothing short of miraculous in an American society so deeply fragmented along sectional, economic, class, racial and ethnic lines. Fundamental change in education could not, of course, have been achieved in a sociological vacuum. It had to be part of a national crusade to transform the inner cities into decent places to live. And this meant giving far greater attention to other public purposes, such as health care, housing and environmental protection.

At the same time that a steady move toward equality was required, there needed to be a sound population policy. This would ultimately be required anyway on ecological grounds, but was a more immediate political necessity because of the unique racial and class structure of American society. Without a positive, vigorously-enforced population policy, there would be a steady demographic shift in favor of the minorities. It was precisely the rapid growth of deprived, frustrated, alienated and increasingly unassimilable minorities which caused the breakup. A consistent and effective population policy would also, of course, have required a firm immigration policy allowing far fewer legal immigrants and no illegal immigrants.

The U.S. was not the only country with a great gap between rich and poor, but its situation in socio-economic terms was quite different from that of most other advanced countries. More than any other major country, the U.S. needed to make a national commitment to work actively and steadily toward equality and justice for all, for in the U.S. there were minorities the size of whole nations which were separated from the mainstream culture by both class and race, and which were a rapidly growing portion of the whole population. The fact is, the class differences which existed in Europe and East Asia were easier to bridge than the race/ethnic/class differences in the U.S. A Frenchman, German, Korean or Japanese who earned no more than the minimum wage of his country led a difficult life to be sure, but at least it could be a tolerable one with reasonable safety, adequate health care and a reasonable hope that an equal and high-quality educational system would offer genuine social mobility for his children. But an African-American or Hispanic earning the minimum wage was likely to have no alternative to living in a ghetto or barrio where he was in constant peril from street crime and surrounded by utter social and cultural degradation. And he would know that barring very unusual good fortune, his children would likewise remain trapped.

The sad fact was that the U.S., which for nearly 200 years had prided itself on being the most egalitarian and socially mobile of societies, had by the latter part of the 20th Century become the least equal and one of the least socially mobile among the industrialized countries. This was due mainly to a large and growing number of people being inescapably trapped in degradation by their racial or ethnic background. This being so, by 2016 the breakup of the United States along racial and ethnic lines can be said to have become very difficult to avoid, if not quite inevitable.